For Inge, Ryan, Gwen and Ethan — K.S.

For Beaux — K.C.

The Hidden Wisdom of Animals © 2025 Quarto Publishing plc. Text © 2025 Kate Siber. Illustrations © 2025 Kaitlynn Copithorne.

First Published in 2025 by Wide Eyed Editions, an imprint of The Quarto Group.
1 Triptych Place, London, SE1 9SH, United Kingdom.
T (0)20 7700 6700 F (0)20 7700 8066 www.Quarto.com
EEA Representation, WTS Tax d.o.o., Žanova ulica 3, 4000 Kranj, Slovenia.

The right of Kaitlynn Copithorne to be identified as the illustrator and Kate Siber to be identified as the author of this work has been asserted by them in accordance with the Copyright, Designs and Patents Act, 1988 (United Kingdom).

All rights reserved.

No part of this publication may be reproduced, stored in a retrieval system, or transmitted, in any form, or by any means, electrical, mechanical, photocopying, recording or otherwise without the prior written permission of the publisher or a licence permitting restricted copying.

A catalogue record for this book is available from the British Library.

ISBN 978-0-7112-9476-9

The illustrations were created digitally.
Set in Branders, Broadsheet, Brother 1816 Printed, Bookmania and Roca.

Designer: Sasha Moxon
Editor: Claire Saunders
Consultant: Barbara Taylor
Production Controller: Robin Boothroyd
Commissioning Editor: Debbie Foy
Art Director: Karissa Santos
Publisher: Debbie Foy

Manufactured in Guangdong, China TT202506

9 8 7 6 5 4 3 2 1

Kate Siber *Kaitlynn Copithorne*

The HIDDEN WISDOM of ANIMALS

Surprising Things
We Can Learn
From Nature

WIDE EYED EDITIONS

CONTENTS

Introduction	8
Owls	10
Squirrels	12
Pigeons	14
Sloths	16
Spiders	18
Dolphins	20
Fireflies	22
Giant pandas	24
Octopuses	26
Flies	30
Jellyfish	32
Elephants	34
Hares	36
Bears	38
Hummingbirds	40
Salmon	42
Vultures	44
Snakes	46
Lynx	48
Flamingos	50
Lobsters	52
Tasmanian devils	54
Lions	56

Monarch butterflies	58
Crickets	62
Turtles	64
Penguins	66
Slugs	68
Wolves	70
Eagles	72
Oysters	74
Crocodiles	76
Foxes	78
Frogs	82
Arctic terns	84
Chimpanzees	86
Tuatara	88
Crows	90
Otters	92
Whale sharks	94
Ants	96
Bees	98
Bats	100
Koalas	102
The Gift of Being Human	104
Caring for Our Family of Beings	106
Index	108

THE HIDDEN WISDOM OF ANIMALS

Whether you live in a city or the countryside, in Boston, Berlin or Timbuktu, nature is all around you! Look closely . . . incredible creatures of all shapes and sizes live and roam on nearly every patch of this planet we call home. Over there, a crow sits watching you from a tree. A slug glides on the ground beneath your feet. A spider hangs from a thread and a red fox is sleeping in the bushes near your shed.

Right under your nose, you might begin to notice a hidden world of magic and wonder. There are so many great things wildlife can teach us. Each creature has beautiful gifts to share, if only we take a moment to see.

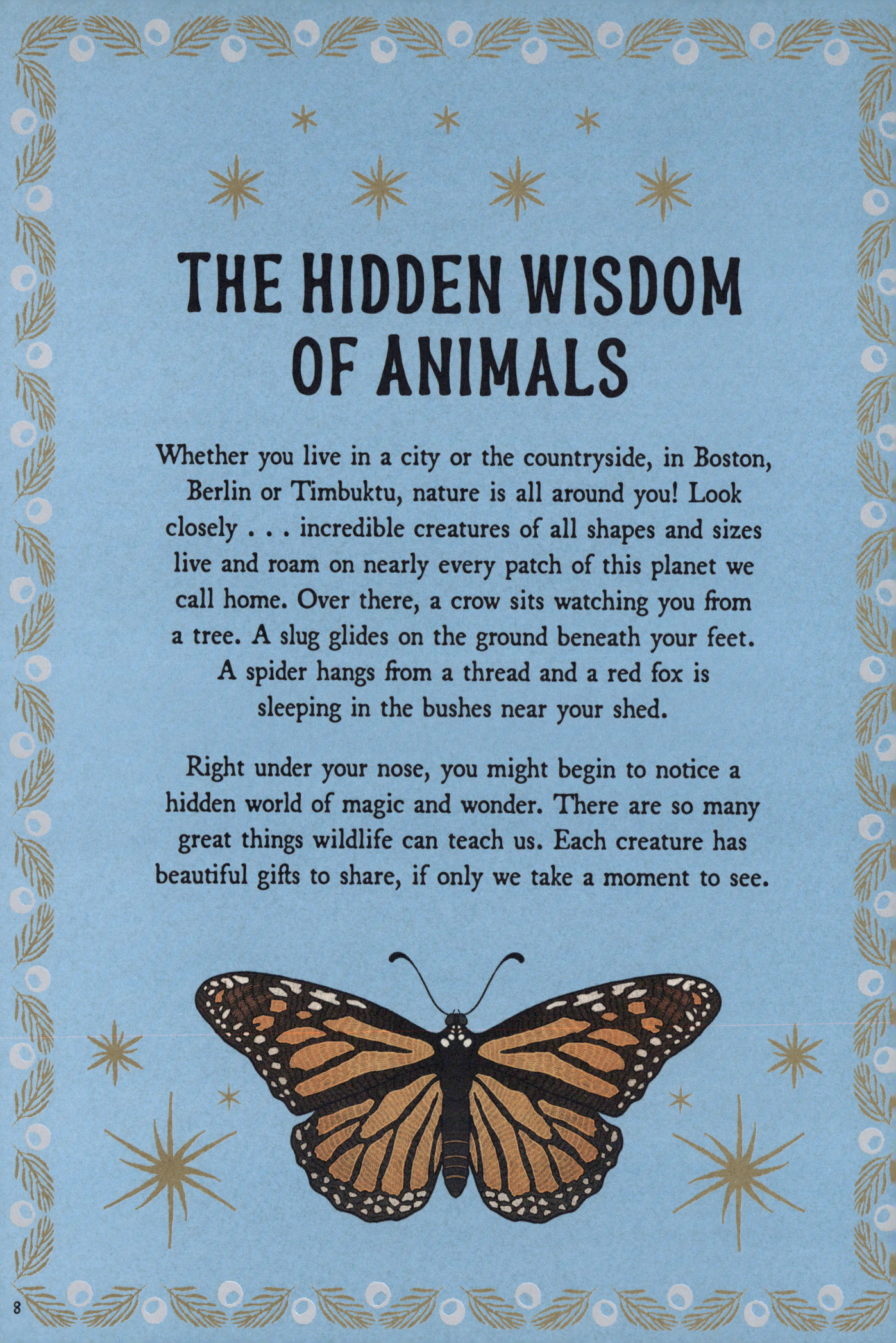

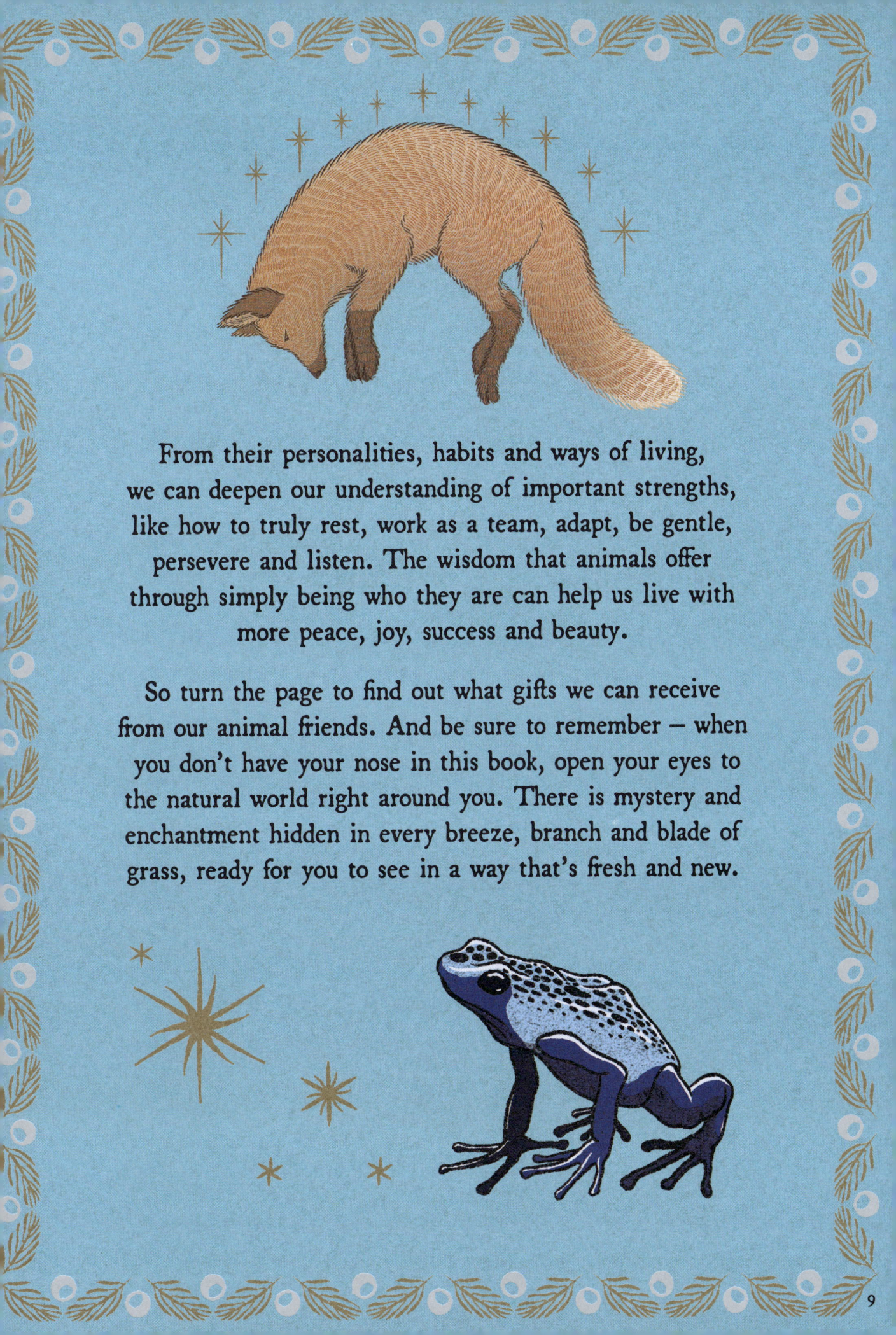

From their personalities, habits and ways of living, we can deepen our understanding of important strengths, like how to truly rest, work as a team, adapt, be gentle, persevere and listen. The wisdom that animals offer through simply being who they are can help us live with more peace, joy, success and beauty.

So turn the page to find out what gifts we can receive from our animal friends. And be sure to remember — when you don't have your nose in this book, open your eyes to the natural world right around you. There is mystery and enchantment hidden in every breeze, branch and blade of grass, ready for you to see in a way that's fresh and new.

OWLS
know how to listen

In the quietest hour of night, a stirring *who-who-who* resounds through the trees. It's the call of an owl – a creature of darkness, a seer through the black. When daylight dims, listen for hoots, chirps and barks that ring through deserts, meadows, wetlands and cities. In the gloom of twilit forests, under the cover of stars, search for moonbeams in big glowing eyes.

To travel through the night on fleet wings, you must have sharp senses. Some owls' eyes are the same size as their brains. Many are so large, you can peer into an ear and see the edge of an eyeball. Snowy owls can spy a lemming move from more than half a mile away. But these beings of hushed wings may be best known for their listening.

Barn owls can hunt by sound alone in meadows and pastures on moonless nights – they have some of the best-known hearing of anything that breathes. Great grey owls hunt blind, flying low, listening for the faintest rustling of a mouse beneath snow.

What is the secret of great listening? In the case of the barn owl, it may be her perfect ears, which perch on different sides of her head – one up, one down, one true, one askew. Like many owls, her heart-shaped face catches sound like a dish, and she can turn her head clear behind her in either direction. Blinking and turning, she can pay really close attention. Silence helps too. The elf owl, so tiny he could fit in your palm, is the smallest known raptor of any. Even in the extra quiet Sonoran Desert of North America, his silky soft feathers slice through the breeze with barely a noise.

Beings who see, hear or know more than others are often revered and sometimes feared. For some human cultures, from the Pima of North America to the Sicilians of Europe, owls foretold death. Their night-moans and hoots brought terror to quivering hearts. Yet owls have also been symbols of wisdom and knowledge. An owl accompanied the Greek goddess Athena, keeper of wisdom, and whispered great truths and secrets in her ear. A beautiful white owl graces the shoulder of Maa Lakshmi, the Hindu goddess of wisdom, health and good fortune.

Being able to pay attention, observe, see clearly and listen helps us understand the world and light the way for others. In what ways are you like the owl – a wise soul who sees what is hidden, a keeper of secrets and a wizard of deep listening?

SQUIRRELS
know how to plan ahead

When your home is a tree, you think fast on your feet. From the rainforests of Thailand to the cities of England, tree squirrels use their big bushy tails for balance. These marvellous mammals leap through the branches and bound between trunks, their homes as much air as tree bough and twig. Some turn their feet all the way around to dangle off branches in search of seeds or nuts. (They'll eat just about anything, from fruit and leaves to fungi and bugs.)

Beyond their trapeze-artist daring, however, another quality suits squirrels for life in the trees: their cleverness of thinking ahead. Whether in the tropics or cooler forests, trees go through cycles of producing and resting. Squirrels know there will be times when their food source is tested. That's why they gather enough to save for later.

Consider red squirrels and Douglas squirrels, who live in the land of changing seasons and gather pinecones into piles called 'middens.' Some stretch as large as 3 metres wide. They defend their troves from sneaky marauders and even pass their collections to the next generation. Grey squirrels take a different approach, digging holes by the hundred. Imagine looking for so many buried acorns! Amazingly, they remember 90 per cent of the locations.

Even in wilds where winter is absent, many squirrels save for later. The Indian giant squirrel, as big as a puppy, lives in misty cloud forests and hoards seeds in the treetops. Indochinese flying squirrels carve grooves in their nuts and wedge them between branches.

Do you, like squirrels, have the gift of thinking ahead? Do you consider what's coming and act wisely now? Squirrels show us it can be the key to survival. In cooler climates, they work hard all autumn, jumping and digging, leaping and nibbling. When snow returns, they curl up in their nest or den – warm, cosy and well fed.

PIGEONS
know how to come home

A calming coo in the park, the clack of wing flaps on your street – pigeons are peaceful beings, always there but so rarely truly seen. They may seem ordinary as they strut and bob and murmur on roads and doorsteps. But little do most of us know, they are secret heroes. Look beyond their shimmery necks, multicoloured feathers and three-lidded eyes. Their gift is invisible because it's inside: the homing instinct.

By six weeks of age, pigeons know their homes well. When released far away, they flap straight back to their coops, committed to the important task of returning. Just about nothing can stop them – not sparrowhawks, snakes, smoke, fierce winds nor gunfire. Even when they're more than a thousand kilometres away, even when they're blindfolded or can't quite hear, they return to the place they know.

To discover how their inner compass works, we have followed them by plane and helicopter. We have strapped packs to their backs. And still we do not know their secrets.

They might tune to the electromagnetic field of Earth or find their way by smell or landmarks, or a combination of cues. But even though we don't understand, we have admired their talents for thousands of years. Images of pigeons appear in ancient Egyptian tombs and on Mesopotamian clay tablets. Akbar, a Mughal emperor of South Asia, kept 20,000 of these birds in the sixteenth century. Pigeons have carried messages for us, braving bombs in World War II and, so legend tells, delivering news of the conquest of Gaul to ancient Rome.

You also know how to find your way back home. Home is sometimes a place, sometimes people and sometimes a feeling. Home, they say, is where the heart is, where you feel safe and at ease. No matter how far you may one day go, how long you are gone or how dimly you remember the path of return, you too are a navigator through the clouds. Find your way back to that spot or those folks or that feeling within, just like the birds who travel the breezes, listening to the call of the place they belong.

SLOTHS
know how to slow down

Sometimes... there is something to be gained from doing not much at all... How slow can you go? How little can you do? Just ask a sloth, an expert in dawdling.

In the dripping rainforests of Central and South America, ringing with chirps and croaks and croons, look closely among the trees – a sloth may be hanging quite happily among the leaves. Sleeping for twelve hours a day and never in a hurry, they progress through the treetops at the rate of oozing honey. Imagine what it must be like to have nowhere to be!

When Europeans first met these animals, they were appalled by their pace. In 1749, a French naturalist called them stupid, lazy and a disgrace. But sloths have a secret that some people can't understand. Their slowness is really a talent. For thirty million years, they have moved quietly and carefully, branch by branch, stone by stone, cleverly conserving their energy. In fact, everything they do matches their leisurely ways: to digest a single leaf, it takes as many as thirty whole days.

While everyone else hustles about, the sloth knows that in slowness there can be safety and success. Quiet and serene, sloths harbour whole villages of fungi, algae and moths in their fur. Smelling like forest and green like the trees, in stillness, the sloth can hide in plain sight. A harpy eagle soars amid the canopy... A jaguar stalks through the muck... but the sloth is safe while making no effort.

What would it be like to slow down a bit, too?

How would it be to relax in a tree, savouring a leaf or listening to the forest's symphony?

Pause, notice, enjoy, breathe...

In this world of speed and bustle, what if – for just a little while – you could do much more by doing nothing at all?

Sometimes, all you need to succeed is to simply just *be*.

SPIDERS
know how to create

Deep in the southwest United States, the Diné, also known as Navajo, share the story of Spider Woman, who long ago taught the people how to weave. Through her gift of creation, the people learned how to clothe and care for themselves. Across the world in the Pacific Ocean, the islanders of Kiribati speak of Nareau, the spider who created the world from nothing, when there was no land or light. When new earth is born from the spouting of volcanoes, spiders are often the very first creatures to arrive.

Since the beginning of time, the eight-legged ones have entranced us with their ability to create something from nothing. From organs named spinnerets, they whirl their great threads, highly elastic and stronger than steel. But who could dream up all the wondrous ways they use them?

The Bolas spider creates a silk lasso with a glob of glue on the end, whipping it through the air to catch fluttering moths. Net-casting spiders weave miniature nets that shimmer silver-blue, which they hold between their legs and toss at passing crickets. Other spiders use their silk as a sail. Climbing to a tall spot, they stretch their spinnerets skyward and let loose a long strand. When a breeze arrives, it whisks them away to distant lands. In ponds and streams across Europe and Asia, diving bell spiders sculpt silvery globes and fill them with air. Then, with their bubble submerged beneath the surface, they spend almost their whole lives underwater.

But among all the glorious silk spinners' arts, webs might be the most marvellous. Some spiders create flat sheets or mazes of threads.

diving bell spider

orb weaver

Look closely to
see webs in a
triangle, a tangle,
an 'H' or a ladder.

In the forests of South
America, tiny spiders
work together to make
webs as big as buses. On the
island of Madagascar, the world's
largest webs stretch 20 metres or
more across rivers. The orb weavers seem
to specialize in the spectacular. Living in the tropics,
they adorn their webs with spirals, circles and zigzags. No one
quite knows why. Some think these decorations, called stabilimenta, mimic
flowers and attract prey. Others think they make spiders look larger to
predators or prevent clumsy beings like us from tearing them away.

We too have the ability to create new things – a watercolour,
a song, a dance or a poem. Whether your medium is paint, clay,
fabric or your body, every human can give birth to new gifts.
What is the unique way that you like to create?
Trust that you too have the ability to make,
and, like the silk-spinning ones,
fashion the world into a
more beautiful place.

net-casting spider

DOLPHINS
know how to play

Just beneath the surface of a Tahitian lagoon, a pod of dolphins ripples through the sea, sunbeams speckling their smooth grey backs. They leap and flip and spin. Beneath the swells, they swirl in what seems like an elegant tango. In deeper waters, they find a pufferfish to play with, tossing her back and forth like a ball. Clicking, chattering and squeaking, they whirl away, disappearing like phantoms into the great blue beyond.

It's a gift to glimpse these citizens of the sea, don't you think? Ship captains for centuries have welcomed the sight of dolphins leaping in their bow waves. The ancient Greeks thought of them as good omens, and pictures of gods riding dolphins appear on their coins and sculptures. Like us, these mammals breathe air. Like us, they nurse their young. And, like us, they appear to have playful, inquisitive spirits.

From our view from the surface, dolphins seem to know how to romp, frolic, caper and cavort. We don't exactly know their mission or purpose, but dolphins are often seen riding waves near surfers. They toss seaweed between them and balance it on their snouts. They play catch with sea stars, fish, birds or even sharks. Some play-fight or wrestle or chase each other around. Others experiment with noise like a game – listen for their underwater barks, squawks and whistles. From play, dolphins learn how to move, hunt, bond with their friends and maybe even flirt. They work out how to solve problems and challenges. Play might even be a way that they create new traditions.

Among dolphins and humans, youngsters lead the way in play. But if we are wise, our interest in pure fun lasts our whole lives. That's because there are secret gifts to the art of experimenting. It may be the best way to discover new things, learn our hidden talents and expand our minds. How imaginative can you get? What new game, sport or craft can you try? What purpose-free adventure can you devise?

FIREFLIES
know how to shine from within

B right lights in black forest, who are you?
    A drifting ember?
    An earthbound star?
    A flash of leaf-gold on a summer's eve—
    this is the hour of the firefly.

    Step softly on wet ground,
    wrap yourself in moonless dark.
    Whisper . . .
    behold these beetles' silent codes:
    a wink, a sparkle, a glimmer.

      Fireflies glow from within
      and radiate out,
      lighting the earth just by
      being who they are.

For just a few weeks, they live to find each other.
Each flicker and flutter
a call and response,
a duet of sparks sung over distance.

The firefly knows there's a light inside
that even on the darkest night shines out.
Dear one, remember to look within.
You too are a gleam in a waterfall of light.

Fireflies make light, known as bioluminescence, using special organs on the underside of their bodies. Each species has its own pattern of flashes, which allows the fireflies to find the right mate.

GIANT PANDAS
know how to be two things at once

Black like tree shadows and white like just-fallen snow, the giant panda is often two things at once. In the wild, she's very rare, yet worldwide, her lovable face is known here and there and everywhere.

Crouch low in a thicket of bamboo – there she goes, a safe distance away, waddling alone on a steep ridge where few humans venture. Lush fir trees sway overhead and columns of bamboo clack in the breeze. The air hangs heavy and cool, and golden monkeys glide through the trees. These mountain forests of China are pandas' safe refuge. Fewer than 2,000 survive in the wild. Almost no one has seen one, not even people who have lived here their entire lives.

How is it, dear panda, to be two things at once? You have everything you need to be fierce: sharp claws, a lion's bite, power and size. You weigh up to 150 kilograms! But mostly you are peaceful and gentle, contentedly munching on bamboo. It's only on rare occasions, when you are mating, threatened or protective of cubs, that you show your dangerous side.

The panda is a worldwide symbol of conservation. Breeding programmes and a ban on logging in their home have helped to increase their numbers.

This is partly why you, giant panda, are an inspiration. In China, you are considered a national treasure, and artwork in jade, clay and bronze celebrates your ways. You've become a symbol of the connection between humans and nature, an emblem of peace and friendship. With your contrasts, you show how different things – black and white, fierce and gentle, yin and yang – can balance in harmony.

Even though you are a bear, you appear so cuddly and cute, rolling down hills, somersaulting, swimming, climbing trees, frolicking, snoozing while hanging from a branch. And even though you are big, your pink furless babies are some of the smallest of all – barely the size of a small apple. So thank you, panda, for showing us a way to be two different things at the very same time – rare and everywhere, bulky yet nimble, mild yet wild. May we remember, by your example, that we too can be a living mystery, a precious balance of many different things.

OCTOPUSES
know how to be different

common octopus

Sink 15 metres below the surface of the sea and there in the reef you'll find a wondrous curiosity. An octopus sits in her lair, decorated with old shells. Her two eyes are flat slits, alert and aware. You are not only looking at her, she is looking at you. She sends one of her eight arms out to explore. Before you know it, her suckers are roaming, curious to learn more. Out of interest, she might try to pull you in closer.

Some say octopuses are like aliens on earth, so different and otherworldly they are. Unlike other molluscs, like snails, clams and oysters, they have no hard parts except a beak hidden in their mouth. Made mostly of muscle without a bone in their bodies, these wonderful weirdos can squeeze into spaces scarcely bigger than their eyeballs.

Depending on how you count, they have nine brains and three hearts. They have venom and strength and a big sack of ink, which they shoot in great clouds when an enemy comes near. And instead of red blood, blue liquid streams through their veins.

From the size of a fingernail (a star sucker pygmy) to as wide as a tennis court (a giant Pacific), these creatures roam for prey through the deep seas and sun-speckled coral reefs. Whether hunting or hiding, they are masters of disguise. Take the mimic octopus from Indonesia, who can shift texture, colour and shape to look like a lionfish, flatfish or sea snake. Others change hues to blend in with rock, sand or coral. When threatened, one turns its skin into glowing blue rings. Another grows blotches that look like great stars.

Sometimes we humans fear those who are different – and we are more closely related to dinosaurs than to these shapeless critters. For nearly 1,000 years, Scandinavians swapped tales of the Kraken, an octopus-like monster who sank ships and terrorized sailors. But those who are different can also be admired. In Hawai'i, the god of the ocean, Kanaloa, takes the form of an octopus. In some Indigenous communities on the Pacific Coast of North America, octopuses are symbols of knowledge. Indeed, of all the invertebrates, octopuses are believed to be the very smartest. In captivity, some solve puzzles, play with toys, use tools or travel through mazes.

While octopuses are unique amongst animals, it also seems that each one is unique in herself. Some are feisty and others are shy. Some are careful and others are bold. Just like you and me, octopuses are their own selves and not anyone in between. So no matter what kind of unusual things you do or how different you might be, take heart in knowing that the octopus is out there just being who she is.

FLIES
know how to move their bodies

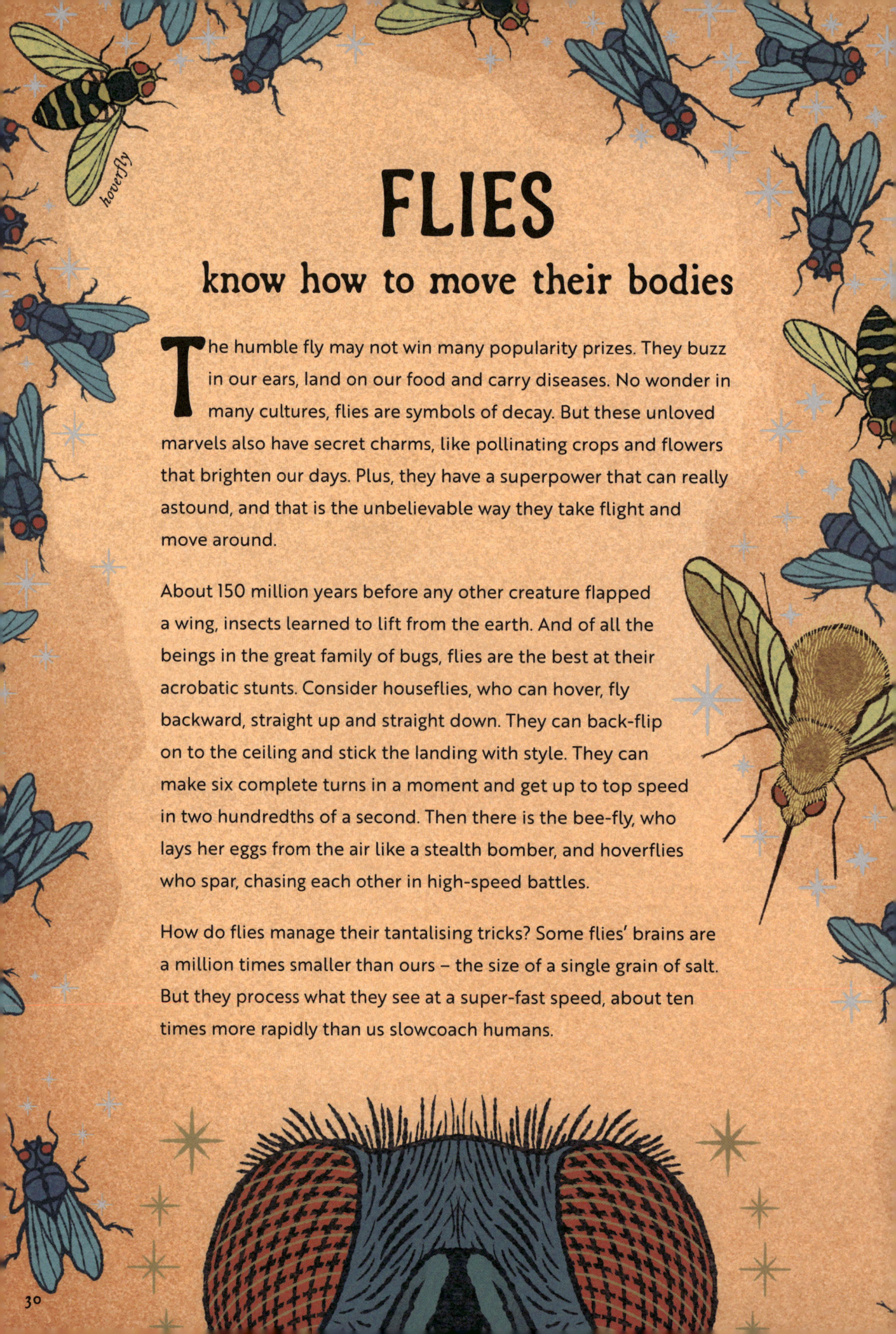

The humble fly may not win many popularity prizes. They buzz in our ears, land on our food and carry diseases. No wonder in many cultures, flies are symbols of decay. But these unloved marvels also have secret charms, like pollinating crops and flowers that brighten our days. Plus, they have a superpower that can really astound, and that is the unbelievable way they take flight and move around.

About 150 million years before any other creature flapped a wing, insects learned to lift from the earth. And of all the beings in the great family of bugs, flies are the best at their acrobatic stunts. Consider houseflies, who can hover, fly backward, straight up and straight down. They can back-flip on to the ceiling and stick the landing with style. They can make six complete turns in a moment and get up to top speed in two hundredths of a second. Then there is the bee-fly, who lays her eggs from the air like a stealth bomber, and hoverflies who spar, chasing each other in high-speed battles.

How do flies manage their tantalising tricks? Some flies' brains are a million times smaller than ours – the size of a single grain of salt. But they process what they see at a super-fast speed, about ten times more rapidly than us slowcoach humans.

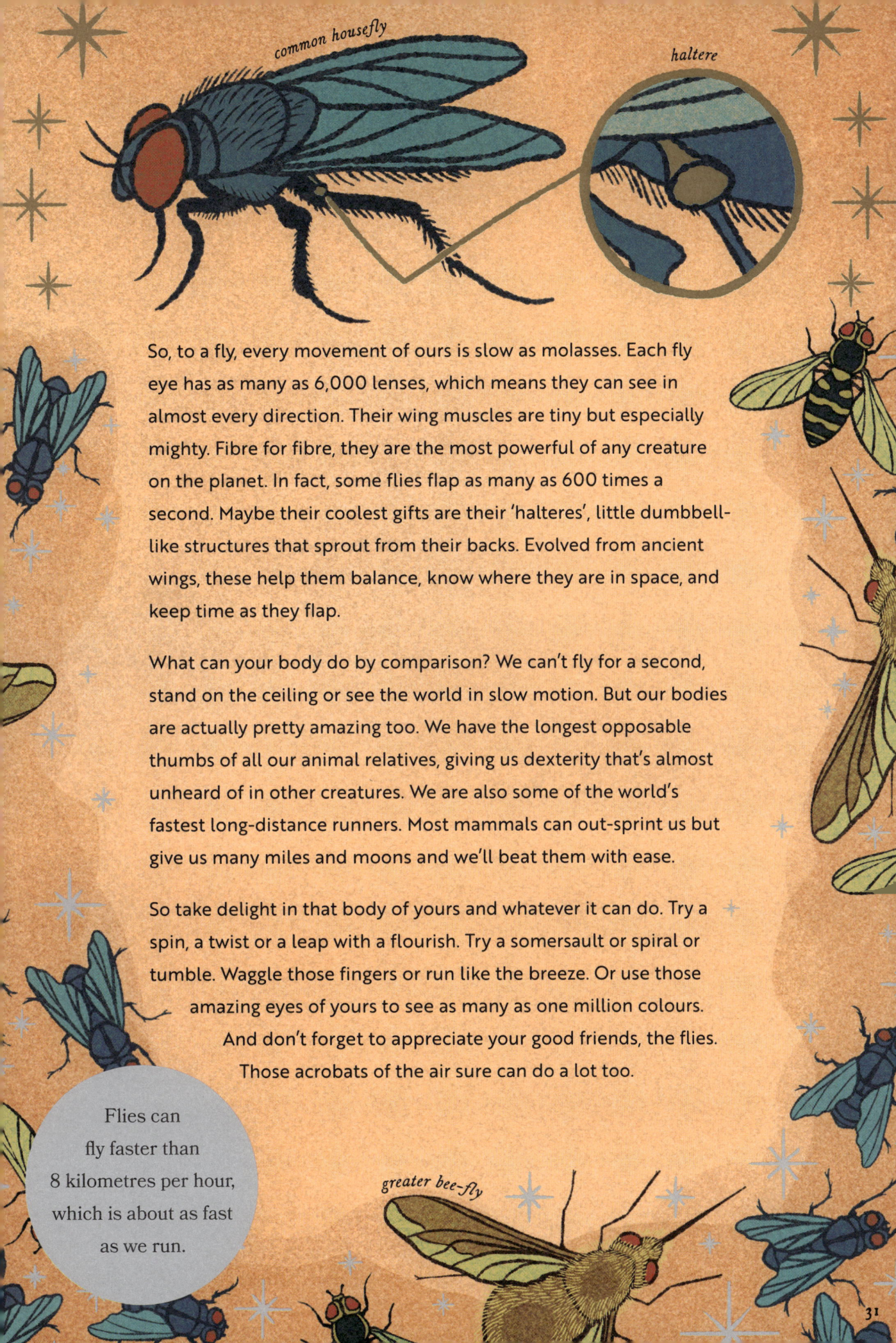

common housefly

haltere

So, to a fly, every movement of ours is slow as molasses. Each fly eye has as many as 6,000 lenses, which means they can see in almost every direction. Their wing muscles are tiny but especially mighty. Fibre for fibre, they are the most powerful of any creature on the planet. In fact, some flies flap as many as 600 times a second. Maybe their coolest gifts are their 'halteres', little dumbbell-like structures that sprout from their backs. Evolved from ancient wings, these help them balance, know where they are in space, and keep time as they flap.

What can your body do by comparison? We can't fly for a second, stand on the ceiling or see the world in slow motion. But our bodies are actually pretty amazing too. We have the longest opposable thumbs of all our animal relatives, giving us dexterity that's almost unheard of in other creatures. We are also some of the world's fastest long-distance runners. Most mammals can out-sprint us but give us many miles and moons and we'll beat them with ease.

So take delight in that body of yours and whatever it can do. Try a spin, a twist or a leap with a flourish. Try a somersault or spiral or tumble. Waggle those fingers or run like the breeze. Or use those amazing eyes of yours to see as many as one million colours. And don't forget to appreciate your good friends, the flies. Those acrobats of the air sure can do a lot too.

Flies can fly faster than 8 kilometres per hour, which is about as fast as we run.

greater bee-fly

JELLYFISH
know how to go with the flow

From the deep, inky ocean
to the flickering shallows,
the jellyfish drifts in its magical forms:
a silvery saucer, a billowing bag,
a shimmering cloud, a travelling moon.

Swimming freely,
body filled with ocean,
living, mostly, for a matter of months,
the jellyfish knows how to go with the flow.

Let this moment be easy, they might say,
if they had brains or bones or notions.
No need to try quite so hard.

Ancient survivor, umbrella of light,
show us how to move with hardly an effort,
to glide with style, to sail and to coast,
to flow with the current in a restful sea.

ELEPHANTS
know how to care for others

Trunk to tail, trunk to tail, a line of elephants lumbers across the great African savannah. A herd of mothers, daughters, aunts and cousins, they wind their way through acacia trees and long waving grasses. They're following their matriarch, who leads them by memory to the promise of water. The sun beats down. A fragrant wind blows. Ears flap and long lashes blink. The largest land mammals of all, these creatures tend to stick together, finding strength in support.

Listen for rumbles, roars, trumpets, grunts, barks and snorts resounding across the land. Elephants are experts at communicating. Through the sensitive pads of their colossal feet, they feel each others' seismic tremors from kilometres away – a network of mysterious messages that we can't even hear, let alone understand. What are they saying, in their elephant way?

Elephants' connections, communication and what many believe is their ability to feel emotion, help them express care. They touch trunks, stand close and brush each other with tails. They console each other, slow down for the weary, help little ones out of the mud and spray dust on one another's wounds. Females of even three or four years of age help care for calves who are not their own, and youngsters follow elders for wisdom, leadership and guidance. Some elephants have been known to help other species, like buffalos, baboons or even us.

Elephants even appear to feel grief after a loss. Some mamas carry around dead calves for days or weeks. After a death, groups gather together, rock and sway. They travel long distances to pay respects to their deceased, stroking white bones or tossing dirt over bodies.

Maybe they understand that they are stronger together. Whether it's seeing, hearing, smelling or feeling, they often seem tuned in to what others are needing. You know how to do this too – to sense what others are feeling, whether they're lively or lonely, glum or glad, and respond with kindness. A gesture, a touch, a word or a smile – this is the glue that keeps us together.

HARES
know how to act quickly

In the hushed woods of winter, high in the mountains, pause, fall silent and look carefully. Over there in the sparkling snow, you can barely see him: a snowshoe hare breathes and blinks. White as the land, still and quiet, all you can see is his one shining eye. He's taking you in to see if you're safe. But move just a millimetre and he's gone in a dash! Speed is the secret of the long-limbed one, who disappears in a flash.

Don't call them rabbits – hares are different, for sure. Larger, with ears stretching to the heavens, hares and jackrabbits live above ground in the open. Across tundra, desert, grasslands and forests, they are experts at staying so still they vanish from view. But their biggest trick is their talent for speed. Their babies – their leverets – are born ready to go, adorned with fur and eyes big and open. In a matter of minutes, they're ready to hop. In hours, they're off in a gallop.

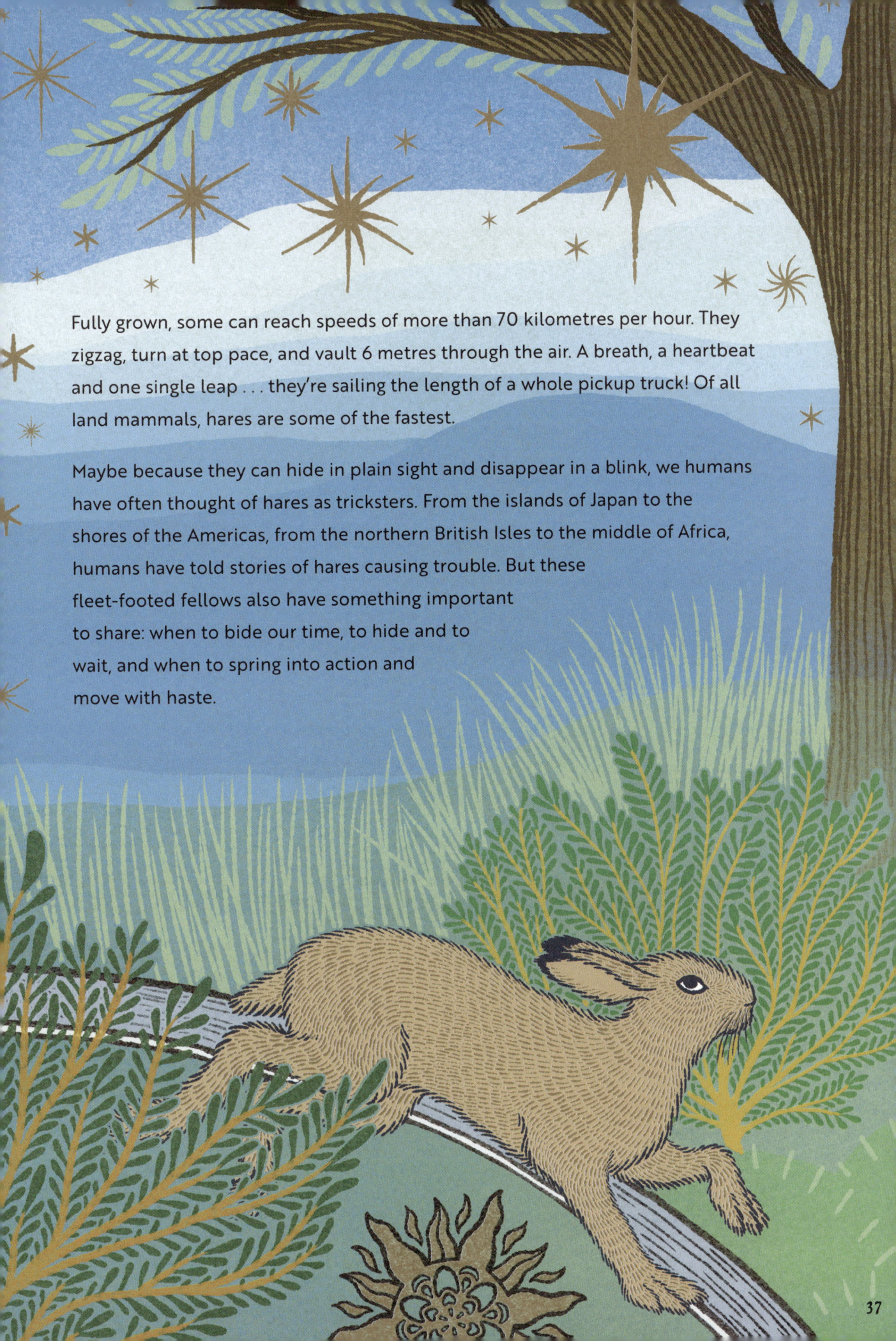

Fully grown, some can reach speeds of more than 70 kilometres per hour. They zigzag, turn at top pace, and vault 6 metres through the air. A breath, a heartbeat and one single leap . . . they're sailing the length of a whole pickup truck! Of all land mammals, hares are some of the fastest.

Maybe because they can hide in plain sight and disappear in a blink, we humans have often thought of hares as tricksters. From the islands of Japan to the shores of the Americas, from the northern British Isles to the middle of Africa, humans have told stories of hares causing trouble. But these fleet-footed fellows also have something important to share: when to bide our time, to hide and to wait, and when to spring into action and move with haste.

BEARS
know how to rest

Autumn is coming and the woods of the north are ablaze in colour. Feel the brisk bite of the autumn air. Watch as the sun dips low in the sky. A faint musky smell hangs in the trees, and piles of berry-filled scat dot the fallen leaves. Tread carefully with awareness and respect – a bear may be wandering near here.

Sure enough, a safe distance from you, a bear appears from behind golden foliage. He knows in his bones that winter is coming. Day by day, warmth is fading. His aim is to grow fat and content, consuming all that he can. Depending on his tastes and what he finds, he'll dine on small mammals, salmon, carrion, bugs, berries and other plants.

There comes a time when his body is big enough, and he is overcome with the urge to find a resting place. Whether his den is a cave, a hollow in a tree, a secret hole somewhere or a bed of leaves, this is his special sanctuary – quiet, dark and deep.

black bear

He turns around three times and lies down for a slumber that can last as long as seven months or, in warmer places, just weeks.

The bear's body temperature dips. His heart slows to fewer than 10 beats per minute. With each breath – about once every 30 seconds – his heart thumps in time. Listen for his great sighing snore. Watch for signs of restless bear-dreams. This is the wondrous phenomenon of deep rest or hibernation.

Bears live in many places. The spectacled bear dwells in South America and the sloth bear wanders the forests of South Asia. But only black and brown bears of Earth's northerly reaches lie down for rests that last a whole season. That's because the land goes dormant, food is scarce and, in their wisdom, bears know it's time to save resources. How clever, to tune the rhythms of your body to the great cycles of nature. The bear seems to know there are times for activity and times for resting.

We humans can sure get stuck in activity. We tire ourselves out – busy, busy, busy. It can be easy to forget that life comes with many different seasons. Maybe you, too, could use your own version of a den – a place to curl up, be quiet and recharge again.

Humans have long felt kinship and interest in bears. In the Chauvet cave in France, people painted pictures of bears more than 30,000 years ago and seemed to specially arrange their bones. Among many Indigenous traditions, the Utes of the American Southwest speak of knowledge gifted by a she-bear and celebrate every year with the Bear Dance. If you need a reminder of the wise ways of the bear, in the Northern Hemisphere, look up after dark. Among all the pinpricks of light, the Ursa Major (Great Bear) and Ursa Minor (Little Bear) constellations always look down and wish you goodnight.

HUMMINGBIRDS
know how to be fierce

Long-nosed flower-kissers,
lightning-quick flyers,
daring dive-bombers,
hummingbirds live their lives
in blazing fast-forward.

Buzzing and whirring,
hovering and darting,
swooping upside down,
they're mini bundles of courage.

Hummers are the smallest and lightest of birds,
some weighing no more than a coin,
some babies the size of a bean.

The Aztecs, who ruled parts of Mexico 500 years ago, believed warriors turned into hummingbirds when they died. Their swords became hummers' long beaks.

Costumed in iridescent rainbow glitter,
with hollow bones and airy feathers,
they have giant hearts that beat
more than a thousand times every minute.

They look so brave as they chase each other in heroic battles
and stand up to creatures great and grim –
    geese, eagles, hawks and herons.
      But toughness is a task that
        comes with the tiny.
          Ounce for ounce, they may be
            the fiercest of all:
              proof that strength
                isn't about size, but spirit.

SALMON
know how to persevere

On their long, winding way home from sea to stream, salmon leap up waterfalls, fight rapids churning and white, and swim against currents for hundreds or thousands of kilometres. They squirm through beaver dams – or jump and flop right over – and even push through heaps of gravel.

Salmon live in the ocean for most of their lives, but to mate, they embark on a heroic journey, returning to the place they were born in a freshwater stream. How do they know where to go and when? They have a set of instructions passed down through their genes, and when the time is right to spawn, they feel the urge – deep in their bodies – to migrate. They tune in to the magnetic field of Earth, and a superior sense of smell helps them find the way.

Once they're on the move, seemingly nothing can steer them astray. They face many obstacles on their journey upstream, including human construction, predators, fishermen and the warming of waters through climate change. But amazingly, salmon keep travelling forward, honouring their ancient routes.

The peoples of northern ocean waters – the Ainu of Japan, the Sami of Scandinavia, the Makah, the Umpqua, the Klamath and the Quileute of North America, among many others – know in their bones that salmon are a great gift. The fish feed the animals, the people and even the forests. From their carcasses, nutrients seep deep into water and soil. In ceremonies, rituals, songs and dances, people know to honour, praise and thank the salmon. Without their strength and persistence, the great cycle would end.

Imagine generations of salmon carrying on against the strongest of currents. Perhaps they can inspire you too to make a great effort on a task worth doing.

From the banks of a mighty Pacific river, watch as salmon swim by the thousand. The surface of the water dances with the movements of fish. Look for their shadows twitching in deep pools. Notice their silvery backs quivering in the shallows. They've made it, incredibly, all the way to their destination. This is the miracle of life, against the odds, persevering.

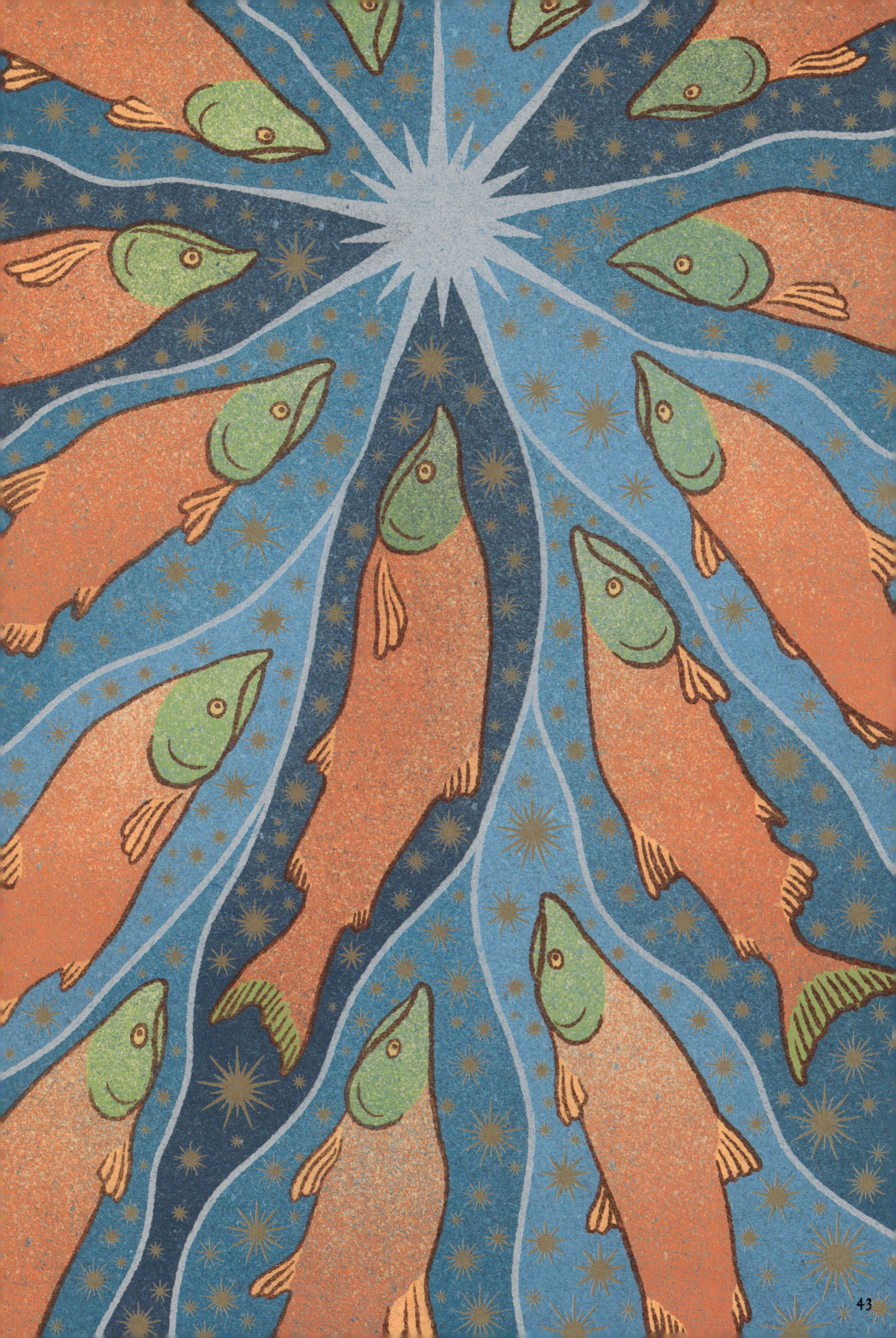

VULTURES
know how to clean up

Up in the sky, hundreds of metres high, spread your glorious wings. Look at the earth unfurl below, a magnificent quilt of blues, browns and greens. Feel the air against your feathers. Outstretched almost 2 metres wide, you soar on the breezes. As warm air rises, you circle, your wings taking occasional deep, slow beats. You're a lofty turkey vulture, doing important work, scanning and smelling for anything dead across the land.

Vultures all over the world, from the Americas to Europe, Asia and Africa, thrive on creatures who have already met their end. With extra-large wings, they catch rides on up-moving thermals and gaze over the earth. A few skim low to catch the scent of the recently departed. Bone-crushing beaks help them tear apart flesh. Strong stomach acid helps them digest anything they swallow, including bacteria and viruses. And many have feather-free heads that help them stay clean when they dive nose-first into a ribcage or belly.

In some cultures, vultures have been considered ugly, spooky symbols of death, perhaps because many have hunched shoulders, wrinkly skin, hooked beaks and dark feathers. It's true, they are the ones who come gracefully looping when you're an animal and the end is near. But for humans, vultures are harmless. In fact, by eating carrion, they clean up the earth for free and don't even complain! Without them, there'd be a whole lot more rats, flies, mites, bacteria and diseases.

So really, everyone could use a vulture around to do the dirty work of a world that produces so many things and throws them out. In streets and parks, mountains and rivers, there are many chances to make the world cleaner. Do you think you could measure up to the great Andean condor, the Egyptian vulture or a Eurasian lammergeier? Soar across the land, with gloves in hand, looking for refuse or scraps to clean away. Or maybe there are things in your very own house that are ready to be tidied up, recycled or discarded. Be a noble vulture, an expert at cleaning up!

turkey vulture

SNAKES
know how to let go

Over there in the grass, a beautiful long snake is curling and twisting in a curious way. It's a special moment, rare and awesome to see: this slender slitherer is ready to shed her skin. Her mood seems sluggish and blue, and her skin turns dull and grey. Her lidless lookers are clear after turning an eerie milky hue. Rubbing her face against a sharp rock, a small tear is torn in that skin of hers. Wiggling and yanking, she peels off the old sheath, turn by turn, scale by scale, like a sock turned inside out. Pretty soon her old skin, delicate and white, is left on the ground as she glides away without a backward glance. With spirit renewed, she looks brand new, her colours crisp and bright.

When shedding, snakes go from stupor to vigour, from listless and lifeless to energetic and free. Maybe that's why Asclepius, the Greco-Roman god of medicine, carried a staff wrapped with a serpent. Healing, you see, isn't just about gaining something new, like strength or health, but is also about what we leave behind.

From the savannahs of South Africa to the tropical waters where sea snakes wriggle, snakes all over the world must shed and let go. Up to four times a year, they're born anew in this way. Whether an adder or mamba, an asp or a garter, moulting allows them to grow bigger. It also lets them discard skin that might be tainted with fungus, parasites or damage.

It's essential but sometimes dangerous stuff, this shedding away. With their vision dulled and their senses slowed, snakes are vulnerable to predators. But if they don't free themselves fully, the risk may be greater. The special scales over their eyes – spectacles – can linger and make them turn blind. If a segment of skin doesn't unglue, it can kill or bind them. So if you have great luck and spot a snake while she's shedding, be sure to honour her sacred operation.

Like snakes, we also learn, develop and let go. Is there something that you didn't realize you already outgrew? Like the snake, is there something you're ready to leave beind? It might be a possession that is old and worn or no longer used. It might be a place you'd like to leave or a hobby or habit you'd like to quit.

We too must moult in order to flourish. When the time has come, be like the snake and let go without lingering.

LYNX
know how to be calm

The lynx was born for remote kingdoms of deep, deep snow. Across the icy wildernesses of the great far north, Canada lynx stalk gracefully over the hills and hollows of vast frozen forests.

With supreme hearing and vision, they hunt in the shadows.
With enormous paws, they stay afloat in white fluff.
With thick, dense fur, they are untouched by wintry wind.

Watch for their telltale tufted ears and their slender bodies. They are as tall as medium-size dogs but lanky and lean, ready to sprint or spring or pounce. If you are lucky enough to spot a lynx, remember that it's because he's letting you see him. He may have seen you a dozen times without you even noticing. But even though lynx may seem scarce and secretive, perhaps even shy, many are calm and unafraid.

The Canada lynx may be particularly serene, whether alone in the wild in the harshest of climates, or even near an intrepid human. In northern Maine, people have told stories of fishing off bridges only to turn around to see a lynx saunter by, chill and aloof. Canoeists have spotted them basking in the sun on lakeshores, content and undisturbed by the sounds of dripping paddles. Even when caught in scientists' traps, Canada lynx don't strain or hurt themselves. They sit and rest and watch, waiting for an opportunity to escape.

Canada lynx

Canada lynx live in North America and Eurasian lynx live in Europe and Asia, while the rare Iberian lynx dwells in woodlands in Spain and Portugal.

Maybe lynx's natural tranquility is what allows them to not waste energy struggling against circumstances. They show the same great patience while hunting, as they wait to ambush their prey. The lynx stays composed and collected in the face of challenge. In moments of worry or when you feel nervous, remember the majestic lynx, who prowls silver moon-shadows in howling winds. Breathe and blink and settle, even if just for a minute, into that unruffled cat-like calm.

FLAMINGOS
know how to be flamboyant

Are you ever afraid to show your true colours?

The flamingo doesn't seem too self-conscious.

He's the colour of sunset, a peach or a tangerine, the hue of cotton candy, or an unstoppable flame.

There on the horizon a river of pink is coming your way, along with the babble and clamour of a thousand birds with something to say.

Be like the flamingo and show your true colours!

You're a graceful cartoon, a honker and hooter, a whooper and flyer, with style and swagger.

Stand on one leg. Flaunt your crooked nose.

Wear whatever colour you like – or maybe all of them at once.
Live life to the fullest, exploring far and wide.
Embrace your inner flamingo –
if you like, be talkative and friendly, and socialise!

Pink, fuchsia, rose or orange,
don't be afraid to let your true self shine.
Sometimes it's ok to take centre stage.
Like the flamingo, you're so fabulous
you can't help but gather applause!

A group of flamingos is called a flamboyance.

LOBSTERS
know how to keep growing

Beneath white-capped waves, on the sandy seafloor, a lobster holds court like a queen with her claws and antennae waving. Watch the patterns of sunbeams dance around her. Hear the bloops and hisses of all the ocean's underwater activities. The lobster, marching confidently with her drifting limbs, can look quite dignified and distinguished.

Crustaceans like lobsters are sometimes seen as simple – after all, they don't have complex brains or feelings.

But one thing they do have that's hard to beat is they don't show many signs of ageing. Lobsters can live more than fifty years (an eternity for invertebrates) and don't seem to slow down, get weaker or lose the drive to mate. And unlike us, they never stop growing. In 1977, a Nova Scotia fisherman caught a record lobster, weighing 20 kilograms and stretching more than a metre – bigger than a toddler!

But life isn't always easy for lobsters. As they continually grow, they must moult their old shells, and sometimes it takes so much energy they die in the effort. On a grassy sea bottom or in a nook in a reef, wiggling out of their shells, they're vulnerable to predators like fish, crabs, octopuses or seals. Male lobsters also fight over females, and females spar over nesting sites. Claws-a-clacking, legs-a-tapping, duelling to and fro, the ten-limbed ones create quite an underwater show. But perhaps one of the keys to their long-lived ways is they can lose parts of themselves – legs, claws, even an eyestalk or antenna – and regrow new ones over time.

Our bodies may stop growing after a while, and we may not be able to sprout a new limb or an eyestalk. But like lobsters, we too, in different ways, keep growing our whole lives. We can expand in wisdom, skills or knowledge.

We can grow our beautiful qualities, like kindness, honesty or humbleness. How do we make sure we keep growing our whole life long? No matter what age, we can be open to new experiences and curious about what we don't yet know.

TASMANIAN DEVILS
know how to be bold

In the murky dark of a Tasmanian forest all covered in ferns, a heart-chilling scream rings through the night. A growl. A shriek. An ear-splitting bark! Who goes there? These are the sounds of the famed ghost of the wood: the Tasmanian devil, who lurks for a meal.

Devils are scarcely bigger than small dogs, but they're filled to the brim with bluster and bite. These Australian mammals have earned their bad reputations from the strength of their jaws and their screeches in the small hours of night. Good at seizing opportunity, they trot through this world eating just about anything they see. They take down animals three times their size and are talented scavengers, pulverizing skin, bones and muscle and leaving nothing behind. Can you imagine devouring 40 per cent of your weight in just one sitting?

People may shudder when they see a devil with a gooey mess all over his face. But you have to respect these creatures for their boldness and courage. They'll charge and spin on a dime and defend their food stashes, growling and crying. Call it what you will – bravado, daring, belligerence or swagger. These lovable beasts are scrappy and proactive. They put themselves out there. Of course, devils also have a softer side and can sometimes be shy. As marsupials, they are good mothers, carrying their infants in a pouch. Some devils who are used to people can even be snuggly and nice.

As a human, it's not good manners to move through the world jostling, pushing, biting and scratching. But there's something to learn from Tasmania's bone-crunching, short-legged wild ones: a fierceness of spirit. As a person, there can be times when it's important to stand up and fight for what's right – with respect and kindness but also strength and an upright spine. Being bold and brave can help you navigate the world's challenges and, even on the darkest night, rise to the occasion.

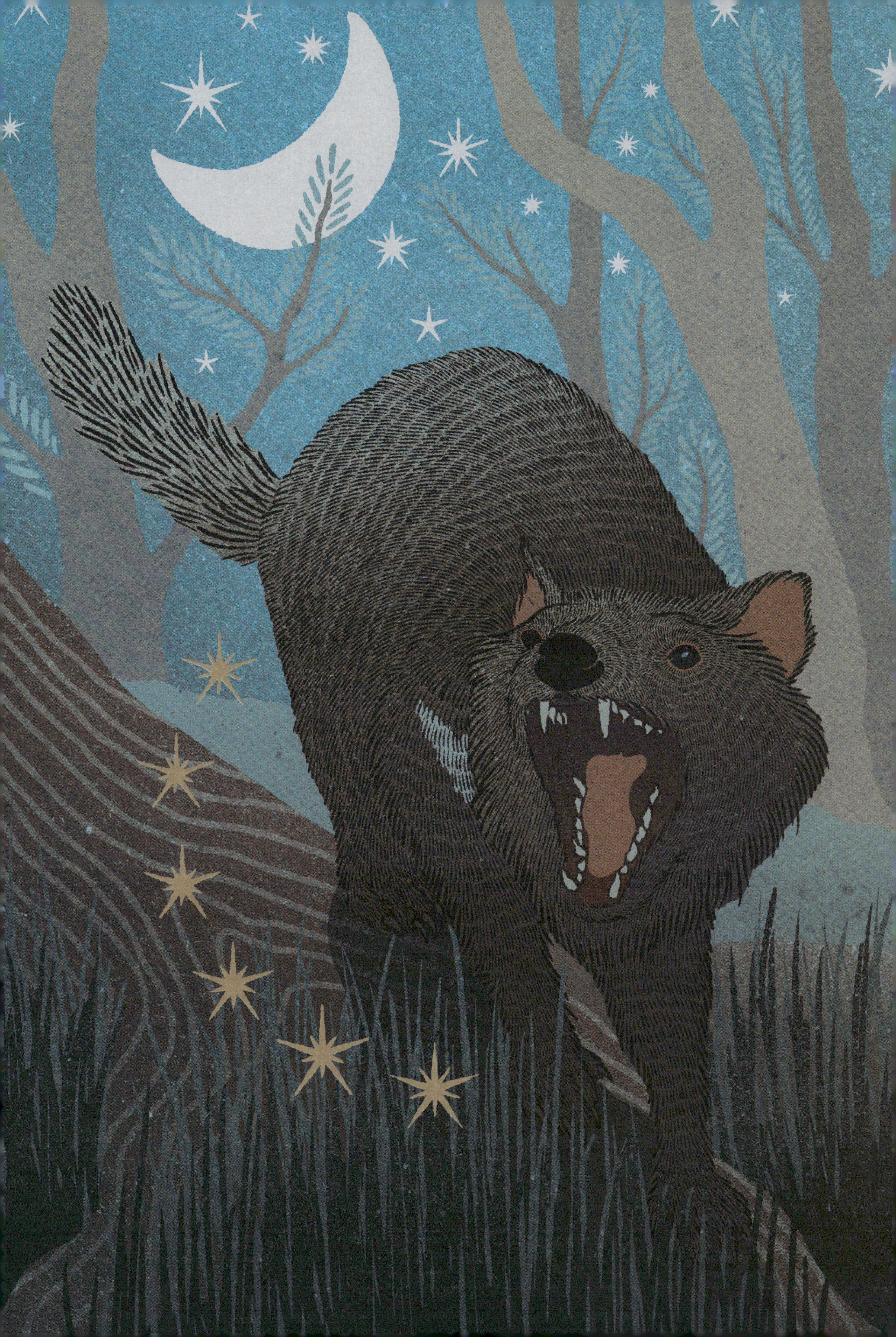

LIONS
know how to be strong

A Maasai warrior, a *Moran*, standing tall, wearing the red robes of his people, gazes over the vast plains of Africa's Serengeti. Since anyone can remember, the Maasai have respected lions for their great strength and power, but they have also feared for the safety of their livestock and family members. Imagine in the quiet of evening, listening to the gut-churning roars of a lion from as far as 8 kilometres away. Would you tremble if you glimpsed a cat that was 2 metres long and more than 180 kilograms, mere steps from your front door?

Humans have long marvelled at the might of these great felines, even far from where they roam in Africa and Asia. If you lived 3,000 years ago in Hattusas, a Hittite city in modern-day Turkey, you might have strolled through the city's majestic gates decorated with carved lions as protectors. Today, you can find stone lions guarding doorways in many Chinese buildings.

Lions' strength comes not only from their muscle-bound bodies and big booming voices, some as loud as thunder. Unusual for cats, much of their success comes from the way they stick together. Groups of lions called prides, made up of females and their cubs, work as a team to defend the group and care for their young. When food is scarce, they hunt prey, whether a zebra, gazelle or wildebeest, for the whole pride. Male groups, known as coalitions, are bands of brothers or best friends. They travel, hunt and nap together for years or even their entire lives. Together, a male coalition and a female pride will hunt for prey to feed the whole group.

Strength isn't only about being big and strong, but about what you do with your power. The Maasai warrior who stands with calm on a great Serengeti hill, is looking for lions. At one time, he and his ancestors killed these cats as a feat of strength and courage, an ancient test of manhood. As lions have dwindled in number, he does something even more courageous. Tracking their whereabouts, gathering observations and standing up for them in his community, he prevents conflicts with humans, becoming their protector instead.

Sekhmet, an ancient Egyptian war goddess, had the head of a lioness and body of a woman. Known as 'she who is powerful', she could cause calamity but was also linked with healing.

MONARCH BUTTERFLIES
know how to share knowledge between generations

The Haudenosaunee of North America know that when you make choices on behalf of your people, you must think not only of yourself and your own family – or even all the people around you – but also about the welfare of all seven generations that follow. Then, they may be able to enjoy the beauty of the earth in the same way we do, or maybe even better. Through this principle of the seven generations, care and wisdom pass down through the decades, from grandparent to grandchild, auntie to nephew, friend to friend.

Monarch butterflies may not speak a language we can understand, but their bodies, like ours, hold special knowledge that they pass down through their families.

In the mountains of Mexico, beams of light stream down through fir groves as a flurry of orange-and-black butterflies take flight – too many to count! Their delicate bodies graze your face and skim your arms. All you can hear are millions of soft wing flaps. So many butterflies crowd the air, they make a mosaic of the sky.

From these fir woods, as well as groves along the California coast, the monarchs make a legendary migration as far as 4,800 kilometres north, and back again. No single butterfly makes it the whole way, but they fly the round-trip in a relay. Each generation pushes farther north, living for a matter of weeks until they lay eggs and pass away. Finally they make it to the northern United States and southern Canada. As cool weather comes, the last generation begins the great return.

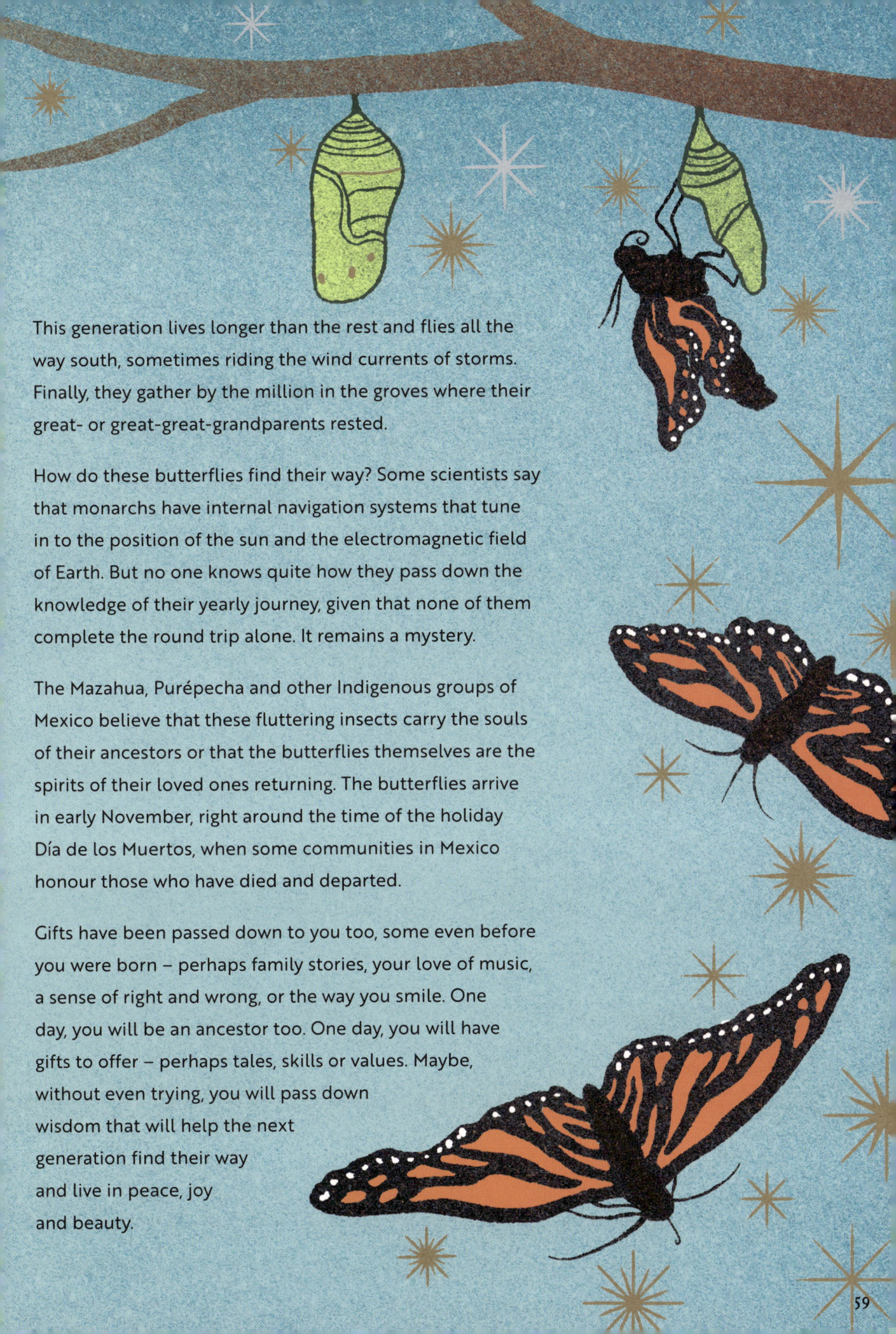

This generation lives longer than the rest and flies all the way south, sometimes riding the wind currents of storms. Finally, they gather by the million in the groves where their great- or great-great-grandparents rested.

How do these butterflies find their way? Some scientists say that monarchs have internal navigation systems that tune in to the position of the sun and the electromagnetic field of Earth. But no one knows quite how they pass down the knowledge of their yearly journey, given that none of them complete the round trip alone. It remains a mystery.

The Mazahua, Purépecha and other Indigenous groups of Mexico believe that these fluttering insects carry the souls of their ancestors or that the butterflies themselves are the spirits of their loved ones returning. The butterflies arrive in early November, right around the time of the holiday Día de los Muertos, when some communities in Mexico honour those who have died and departed.

Gifts have been passed down to you too, some even before you were born – perhaps family stories, your love of music, a sense of right and wrong, or the way you smile. One day, you will be an ancestor too. One day, you will have gifts to offer – perhaps tales, skills or values. Maybe, without even trying, you will pass down wisdom that will help the next generation find their way and live in peace, joy and beauty.

The longest-ranging monarch butterfly ever recorded travelled over 400 kilometres in a single day. The butterflies sometimes gather in swarms so big, they can be seen on radar.

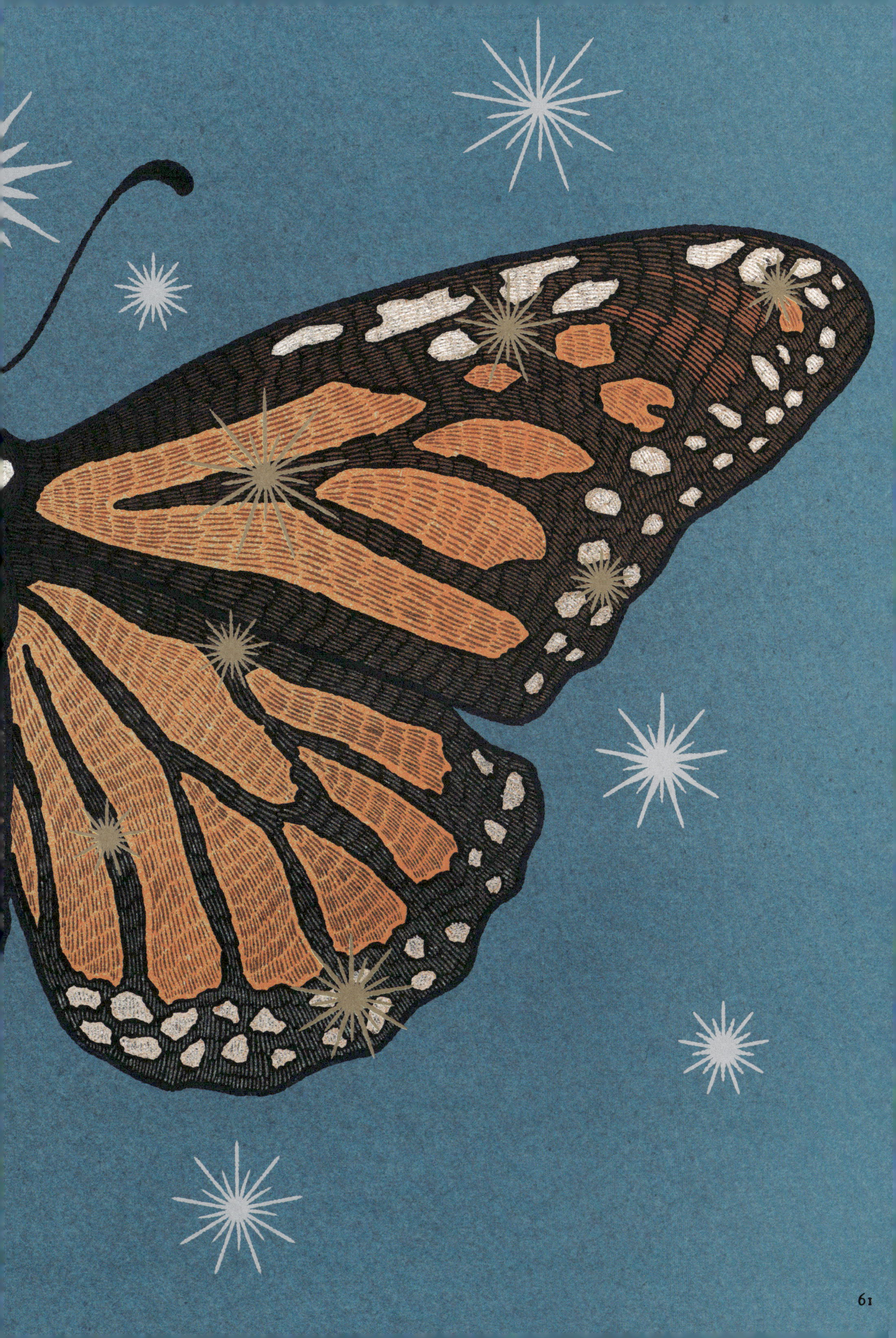

CRICKETS
know how to sing

As day softens into darkness
and Earth sighs and settles,
evening brims with song.

Chirps, cheeps, trills –
cricket sounds collect
into a lullaby for all who listen.

All of those cricket chords over field and wood,
the warbles that blend into the background
of gathering dusk, the thousand notes in the night –
these are the sounds of life renewing itself.

For male crickets find their mates
with this melody, unique to their kind
and born of rubbing wings.

Our voices are also born of our bodies.
We too vibrate and hum.
Through music, we sing the world into being,
celebrate, praise and grieve.

Even if your song is a quiet one sometimes,
even if it's one that only you can hear,
why not sing?

Crickets, as well as other insects like grasshoppers, make sound through 'stridulation', rubbing one body part against another.

TURTLES
know how to protect themselves

The eastern box turtle's shell looks a lot like leaves, but peer just a little more closely . . . There he is, moving slowly, plodding along on a damp forest floor, smelling of flowers and spring. He may look humble, but this turtle has an incredible, magic-like trick. Come too close and he will retract all of his soft, tender parts – head, arms, legs and tail. He not only pulls into his high-domed shell but, with the help of a special hinge, closes it up perfectly tight. You couldn't even sneak a blade of grass inside.

Turtles and tortoises come in many different sizes and forms, but they all have shells that keep them safe from harm. Some shells are soft, and others are hard with spikes or mounds. Some are thick and others are thin. Some even bend! Many turtles can pull totally into their shells while others, like sea turtles, are simply out in the elements.

eastern box turtle

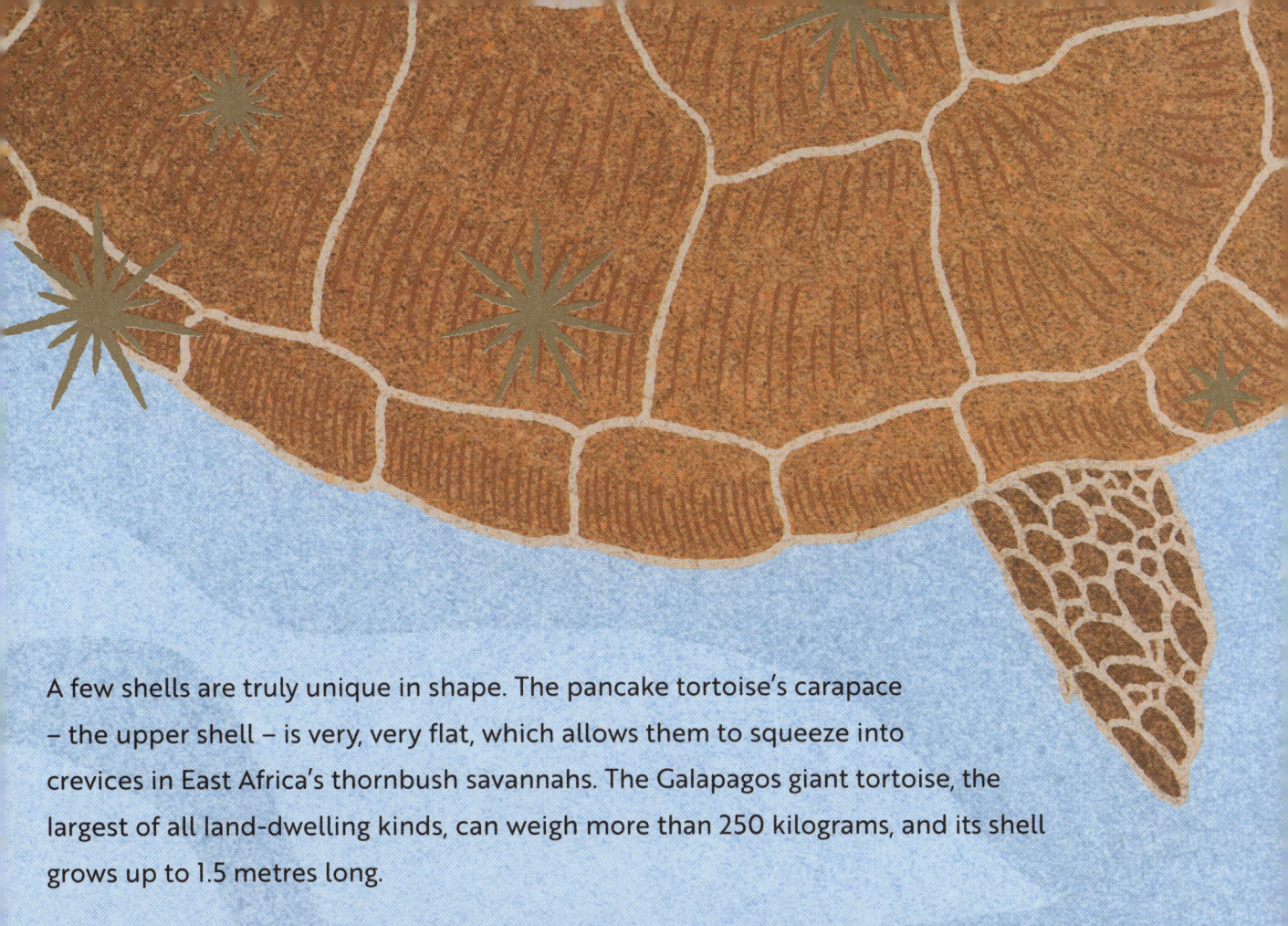

A few shells are truly unique in shape. The pancake tortoise's carapace – the upper shell – is very, very flat, which allows them to squeeze into crevices in East Africa's thornbush savannahs. The Galapagos giant tortoise, the largest of all land-dwelling kinds, can weigh more than 250 kilograms, and its shell grows up to 1.5 metres long.

In Chinese culture, turtles and tortoises are linked with wisdom and longevity, perhaps because they live a very long time. The oldest living land animal is a giant tortoise named Jonathan, originally from the Seychelles. He is believed to have been born in 1832, making him, at last count, over 190 years old. For other peoples, turtles have also been prized for their protective qualities. In the Philippines and New Guinea, artisans have fashioned their shells into armour.

Like turtles, maybe all of us could use a good place to retreat to – or at the very least some personal space. Maybe it's a spot or corner where you feel perfectly safe. Or maybe it's the way you draw a healthy line and don't let people's unkind words or actions seep in. (After all, sometimes their hurtful choices say less about you and more about them.) For turtles, knowing how to protect themselves keeps them alive. Of course, they also know when it's safe to come out, show their soft parts, move freely and thrive.

PENGUINS
know how to be devoted

At the bottom of the planet, in the world's harshest winters, emperor penguins stand over a metre tall but look small in the land of infinite ice. Antarctica is so far south that there are times when the sun doesn't crest the horizon for months and time is filled with darkness. Stars dazzle across the blackest of skies. Storms blow in and out, hurling snow sideways across the unbroken white. Winds gust over 160 kilometres per hour. The temperature drops to -40 degrees Celsius. And still, these penguins huddle together, staying focused on one task: keeping their precious egg warm and protected.

Each penguin father carefully balances his egg on top of his feet, beneath his warm feathered belly. For as long as four months, he doesn't eat, losing up to half of his body weight. He is waiting for his partner to make the journey back from the sea, more than 120 kilometres away, where she has been hunting for food for herself and their chick. She dodges orcas and leopard seals to gulp down fish, krill and squid, then toddles and toboggans on her belly all the way back. Soon, the penguin father will take his turn making the march.

To raise a baby in such a severe spot, these flightless birds commit to each other and to their shared task, even in the world's worst weather. Other penguins live in milder climates, like New Zealand, Africa, South America and the Galapagos Islands, but they too are very good parents. They equally share the duties of creating new life – building a nest, keeping one or two eggs warm, doting on their newborns, hunting for food and defending against predators. Some species and individuals commit to each other not only for a season but for their entire lives.

Devotion helps us accomplish hard things, whether it's raising a penguin chick against the odds or some other activity or cause. What are your vows, promises or pledges? What do you keep returning to with faith and love? Whether it's care for one's family, commitment to a goal or a passion for helping others, we can learn from the penguin that amazing good can come from being courageously devoted.

When an emperor penguin father says goodbye to his chick, he sings songs. Upon his return, they'll be able to find each other by sound.

banana slug

> A group of slugs is known as a cornucopia.

SLUGS
know how to belong

Imagine the world from a slug's point of view. Grass towers over your head, and the air and ground are alive with scents and flavours. Leaving a trail of silvery slime, you glide across the land, seeing and smelling with two antennae, tasting the soil with two others. A night dweller, an underground traveller, a lover of the damp, you shine in the moonlight. Like a planet that slowly arcs across the night sky, you roam around from dusk till dawn, over moss, stone and leaf, one millimetre at a time.

As beautiful and unique as they are, slugs sometimes get a bad rap. Some books and movies portray them as frightful monsters. Gardeners and farmers bemoan their leaf-munching ways. Because they happen to be cold and slimy, some people think of them as gross. But what the slug can show us is it makes no difference at all if you are considered cute or cool or popular. Slugs, you see, have secret superpowers.

They can crawl over broken glass or even a razor without so much as a scratch. They can shapeshift through the tiniest of spaces to escape or hide. Predators know not to mess with them because of their amazing, tangly mucus-goo. It's not quite a liquid or a solid but a fluid crystal that can be greasy for sliding or sticky like glue. And can you believe slugs have thousands of teeth?

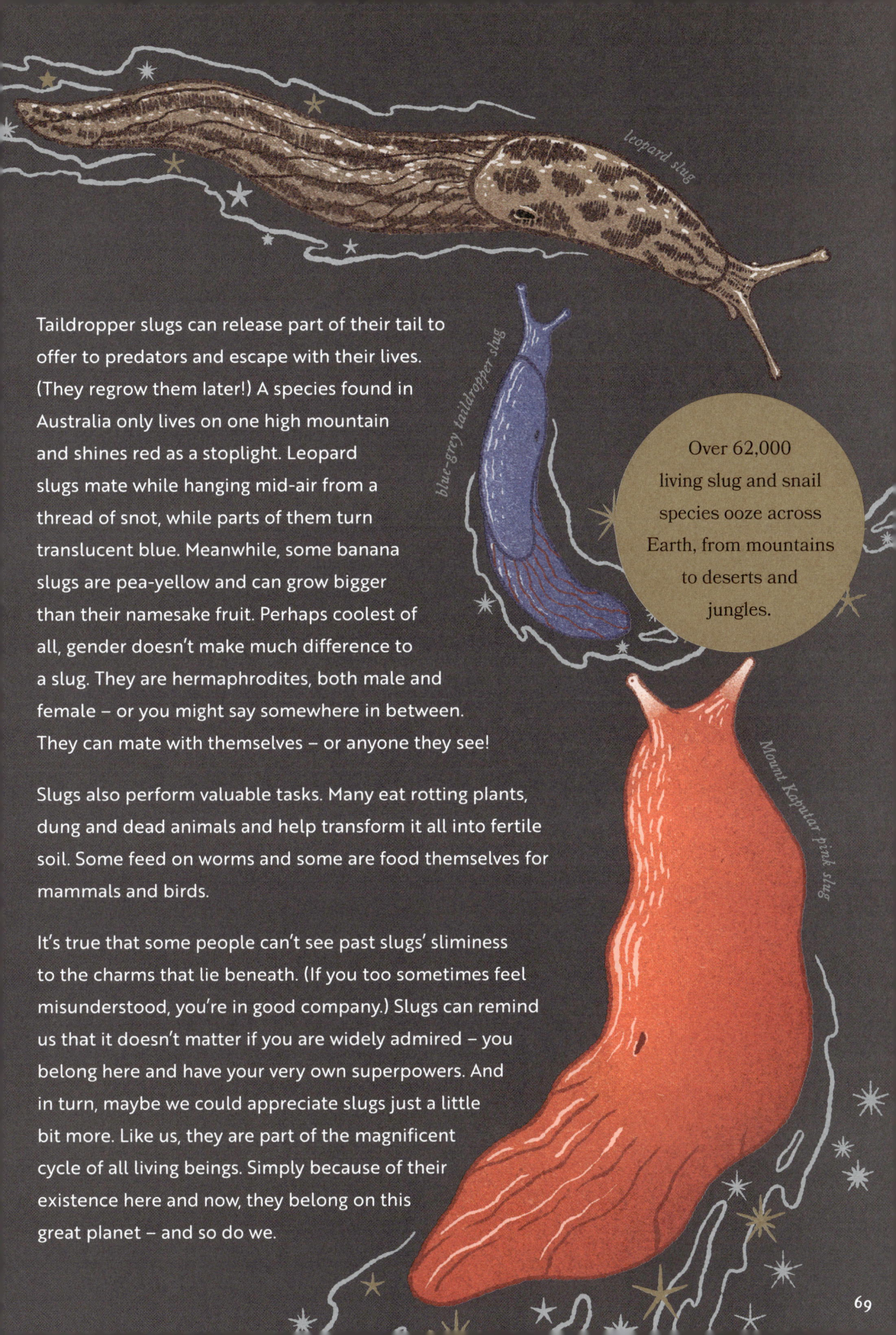

Taildropper slugs can release part of their tail to offer to predators and escape with their lives. (They regrow them later!) A species found in Australia only lives on one high mountain and shines red as a stoplight. Leopard slugs mate while hanging mid-air from a thread of snot, while parts of them turn translucent blue. Meanwhile, some banana slugs are pea-yellow and can grow bigger than their namesake fruit. Perhaps coolest of all, gender doesn't make much difference to a slug. They are hermaphrodites, both male and female – or you might say somewhere in between. They can mate with themselves – or anyone they see!

Slugs also perform valuable tasks. Many eat rotting plants, dung and dead animals and help transform it all into fertile soil. Some feed on worms and some are food themselves for mammals and birds.

It's true that some people can't see past slugs' sliminess to the charms that lie beneath. (If you too sometimes feel misunderstood, you're in good company.) Slugs can remind us that it doesn't matter if you are widely admired – you belong here and have your very own superpowers. And in turn, maybe we could appreciate slugs just a little bit more. Like us, they are part of the magnificent cycle of all living beings. Simply because of their existence here and now, they belong on this great planet – and so do we.

Over 62,000 living slug and snail species ooze across Earth, from mountains to deserts and jungles.

WOLVES
know how to work as a team

Since they can remember, the Anishinaabe have lived in the Great Lakes region of North America. Living on the land together, they see the wolf as a brother or sister. Whatever happens to the Anishinaabe happens to the wolf, they say. Whatever happens to the wolf happens to the Anishinaabe. Many Indigenous peoples of North America credit the wolf with teaching humans to hunt, and Great Plains Nations see them as protectors, guides and teachers.

On the other hand, from France and Germany to Turkey and Greece, people have spun stories of werewolves (humans who turn into wild and scary beasts) for centuries. In European tales like 'The Three Little Pigs' and 'Little Red Riding Hood', wolves are seen as villains. It's true they are predators with big teeth and strong jaws, but in real life they are rarely hostile toward us. While they are powerful, they are also cautious, keeping their distance. Giving them space to roam, can we learn to respect these wild ones and receive the lessons they are offering us?

Like many humans, wolves live in family groups. And by working together, they do the seemingly impossible. Can you imagine how hard it would be to hunt giant animals, like deer, moose, elk, muskox, bison or bighorn sheep, with nothing but wits, claws and teeth? Alone, there would surely be little hope. But through teamwork and clever strategies, such as separating out the sick, the injured, the very young and the very old, wolves are able to hunt animals none of them could bring down solo.

Wolves also work as a team in other parts of their lives. When some are hunting, others are watching the pups. They bring them toys to play with, like antlers, branches or bones. A pack also defends their turf from rivals. They howl together in a spooky wolf chorus that rings through the forest, alerting others that they are a big group and not to be messed with. If you hear wolf calls that make you shiver in the night, remember the lesson of these amazing animals: strength comes through being a team. By working with others, we can accomplish incredible dreams.

Lone wolves are usually not alone for long. Naturally social, they are often looking for a mate and new territory to start a pack of their own.

EAGLES
know how to try again

From high in the treetops of the Peruvian rainforest, a harpy eagle gazes intently with lemon-coloured eyes. Standing around a metre tall with a double crest on his head and talons the size of bear claws, the harpy eagle is one of the most powerful birds in the world. He sits regally, as if he knows he is bird royalty. Spotting movement below, he swoops through gaps in the greenery to ambush prey – maybe a sloth, opossum, anteater or monkey.

But believe it or not, even these magnificent eagles, with their awesome strength, sometimes fail. It may take several tries to grab their prey animals, even when they are within 5 metres of them. More than half the time, the harpy eagle flaps away with empty talons. Eagles, however, don't seem to doubt themselves or what they can do – they simply begin anew.

For some eagles, in times when food isn't plentiful, the need for resilience is even greater. In the wintry wilds of northern Eurasia and North America, golden eagles hunt for small mammals and other prey. Surveying the land, they spot the slightest movements of hares, foxes and other critters using their incredibly sharp vision. Sometimes they are successful only one out of every five tries. They glide and soar, swoop and dive, at times faster than 250 kilometres per hour.

Some predators, especially land mammals, have an easier hunting life. African wild dogs, for example, are famous for succeeding in their hunts as much as 80 per cent of the time. Many things contribute to success, including skills, conditions, teamwork, luck and the willingness to give it one more try. This is what these birds, from the Philippine eagle to the white-tailed eagles of Europe and Asia, can help remind us of: even at the top of the food chain, failure is simply a part of life.

So next time you're feeling discouraged, remember that even the most successful among us only triumph through the great art of beginning again.

harpy eagle

The eagle was a symbol of strength in ancient Rome. Today it is the national symbol of many countries, including Germany, Mexico and Namibia.

OYSTERS
know how to transform their world

Dear Oyster,
We probably don't thank you enough.

Feeding on algae from murky waters,
you filter a bathtub's worth of ocean a day.
Whole bays sparkle because of your work.

When a bothersome speck
enters your shell,
you cover it with a satiny material called nacre
and bring a pearl into the world.
From what's bad, something beautiful is born.

You look so humble, and yet . . .
you transform
both what's inside and what's around:
a grain into a pearl,
cloudy waters into clear.

Grounded like a rock,
tasting like sweet ocean,
you feel rough on the outside
but smooth within.

Could we too learn to transform
what's dirty into what's clean,
what's irritating into something valuable,
what's difficult into wisdom?

Maybe these powers are beyond our reach.

But just imagine –
if we could borrow your gifts, oyster,
we could transform our world.

Both oysters and mussels can create dull pearls, but only pearl oysters can make beads big, even and shiny enough for jewellery.

CROCODILES
know how to be still

In a river calm and deep, a long scaly tail twists and turns.
Crooked teeth flash in the watery gloom.
From sandy shores, a bellow and a dragon-like sigh arise.
Crocodiles are like dreams from an ancient world.

Some crocs grow more than half as long as a bus.
Their bites are the strongest of all known creatures.
Covered in plates of thick, tough armour,
they are the monarchs of murky waters' edges.

One of their great talents is easy to miss.
For many hours, they can be perfectly still.
To not move can seem like nothing,
but from it, much can be gained.
Stillness can help to camouflage,
hide or hunt.

Watching, waiting, gazing . . .
their eyes and nostrils just above water,
crocodiles stay still until prey comes to them.

If you find yourself with time to spare,
see what happens if you too remain unmoving.
Stillness can help you see what you have never noticed before.

What riches might reveal themselves when you settle,
right there in the current of life,
perfectly still, aware,
watching the world pass, one blink at a time?

FOXES
know how to be flexible

Paw by quiet paw, a red fox pads through a field of sparkling snow. She pauses. She cocks her head. She listens. Red foxes have splendid hearing and can detect the scratching of a mouse from at least 12 metres away. *Swish. Ek-ek-ek. Pssht.* Something beneath the snow there moves. Attentive and patient, the fox waits. She crouches. Then, in one fell swoop, she springs into the air and pounces! Headfirst, her bushy tail flying, she dives into the snow with her hind limbs skyward. Almost a metre deep, she pinpoints her meal: a fat, grey mouse.

These ingenious hunting skills are no surprise, for foxes are multi-talented. They are some of the most adaptable of Earth's creatures. They can hunt, scavenge or forage, and eat almost anything, from plants and berries to rodents and lizards – they tend not to be picky.

From South America to the far frozen north, foxes live almost everywhere except Antarctica and swathes of jungle. Some Arctic foxes are great wanderers and have been seen trotting on sea ice close to the North Pole. (They can handle temperatures at least as cold as -50 degrees Celsius without hardly noticing.) In Asia, the Tibetan fox lives on vast plateaus that soar higher than 4,800 metres. The tiny fennec fox, scarcely bigger than a boot, can survive in Africa's harsh and waterless deserts. With its enormous ears, the bat-eared fox listens for prey like termites and beetles. In the Americas, the grey fox can even climb trees.

Foxes adapt and make do and are famous for their cleverness. The English children's book character *Fantastic Mr. Fox* is a food-raiding thief but also quick-witted and charming. In Japanese folklore, *kitsune* are foxes with supernatural powers, said to live for hundreds if not thousands of years. Shifting into different shapes, they are known for their powers of transformation.

bat-eared fox

The red fox may be the most adaptable of all the fox species. They live in woods, tundra, grasslands, deserts and cities. It's possible in fact, that one might live right under your nose – curled up near the garage, perhaps, or nestled by your shed. You might even spot a fox sunbathing in your back garden. Look for them slinking in the shadows or running in broad daylight – foxes are so adaptable they can even shift the hours they're awake.

red fox

The ability to adapt is one of the fox's secrets of success. Like the fox, we too can benefit if we are willing to flex and try a new thing. Sometimes, of course, it's a little uncomfortable. We have our likes and dislikes! But what if you were open to trying something different just this once? Channel the spirit of the fox. Flowing through life with ease could be as simple as the readiness to *stretch*.

FROGS
know how to be sensitive

Trilling, chirping, crooning and croaking, frogs bring symphonies to swamps and streams all over the world. Our amphibious relatives truly amaze with all their different habitats and well-adapted ways. Gliding leaf frogs use webbed feet as parachutes and sail between branches. Namibia's desert rain frog squeaks like a cartoon and survives by squeezing moisture from fog and sand. The blue poison dart frog shines like a living sapphire in steamy jungles, its bright colour warning predators of its skin's deadly toxin. Perhaps most astonishing of all are the glass frogs, whose skin is transparent, allowing everyone to see what's deep inside.

But what these land-and-water dwellers all share is one particular superpower: they have delicate skin that is porous and sensitive. Like us, they breathe through their lungs. But they are also able to drink and breathe through their skin, taking in water and oxygen straight from their environment. Unlike reptiles with their tough exteriors, amphibians' skin isn't a barrier but a means of connection. Frogs, it seems, aren't so separate from what surrounds them.

Because they are a little like sponges, amphibians are often the first to be affected by changes in temperature, pollution or chemicals. This can make them little messengers – warning of things that sooner or later we'll all notice – but it can also make them vulnerable. They are the world's most endangered vertebrates, needing our love and protection.

blue poison dart frog

Many of us are also sensitive beings. If you happen to be especially porous – if sometimes you feel deeply and absorb everything around you – remember that you have a gift that others may need. You may pick up knowledge that lies hidden, secretly sensing things that others don't see. Be proud to be like the glorious frog, who shows us important things that will affect us all. And in turn, maybe we should thank and safeguard our friends, the frogs. We could appreciate their beauty, sensitivity and uniqueness with awe.

golden poison frog

desert rain frog

The golden poison frog stores enough poison within its skin to kill ten people.

ARCTIC TERNS
know how to go the distance

With long, graceful wings that sail on the breeze, airy bones and uncommon perseverance, the Arctic tern makes a great journey from one end of the world all the way to the other.

From the Arctic to Antarctica and back, the tern is in pursuit of the sun as it shifts over the earth with the change in the seasons.

Maybe it's worth travelling more than 40,000 kilometres in a year . . .
Maybe it's worth, over the course of a life,
flying as far as the moon and back several times
to have a chance at eternal summer.

These elegant birds chart their routes
over ocean and ice in curves and zigzags,
feeling their way for winds to ride and fish to eat,
and maybe things that remain mysterious to us.
Sometimes the best path isn't a straight line.

For what are you willing to go a great distance –
to wing over a whole planet with strength
and commitment?

Endurance is terns' gift,
their key to unlocking a sun-blessed life,
in which all their days are full of light.

The Arctic tern's annual migration between the Arctic and Antarctica means it enjoys summer in both regions and sees more daylight than any other animal.

CHIMPANZEES
know how to make peace

Lively, social and loud, chimpanzees bring a party wherever they go. Watch as they swing through the trees and knuckle-walk through forests and grasslands, from Senegal to Tanzania. They spend much of their time together, cackling, hooting and grooming. Covered in hair, they seem so different from us, but in fact they are some of our closest animal relatives.

There are many things we share, and many things we can learn from each other. Chimps are some of the few animals that use tools, cracking nuts with stones and catching termites with twigs. They are full of curiosity and can learn by watching others. Like us, they have different personalities. Some are show-offs or leaders. Others are shy or cautious. They also seem to have complex emotions, even if we don't know quite what they're feeling. And they communicate constantly with barks, roars, grunts and screams, and sometimes take to drumming on trees.

Living in groups, it's almost expected that sooner or later someone will get into a fight. But one thing chimps can show us is how to make up. Even after quite a brawl, chasing each other, beating their chests, screaming and baring their teeth, they come back together and forget it all happened. Their faces look emotional as they hug and set aside differences. Sometimes they'll reach out an upturned palm in a gesture that seems to ask for support or forgiveness. By grooming each other, they bond once again, blowing raspberries with their lips and making *pop-pop-pop* sounds that show they're happy and content.

Conflict is a part of living with others, but it doesn't need to be a big problem. It can lead to more division but also to greater closeness. Inspired by chimps, what if we could be honest and not bottle up our emotions? What if we could hear each other's views, express hurts with respect, and through our ability to disagree and make up, actually deepen our friendships?

Chimp society has a hierarchy. The alpha male becomes the top chimp not because he is a bully but because of his ability to make friends and empathize with others.

TUATARA
know how to survive

Tuatara are the last known member of a whole group of reptiles. They were living on Earth 20 million years before the dinosaurs.

One day, about 65 million years ago, a mountain-sized asteroid going 70,000 kilometres per hour smashed into Earth. The land shook for weeks. Debris flew as far as Mars. Tsunamis towered 1.5 kilometres high and swept away everything on coastlines. Forest fires raged and dust encircled the planet, blocking the sun for months. The tropical Earth cooled, and many of the world's living beings, including most dinosaurs, went extinct. Among those who remained were a group of reptiles named Rhynchocephalia. Today, the very last surviving species of this whole group is the legendary tuatara.

A lizard-like reptile that now lives only on New Zealand's outlying islands, the tuatara is known by the Māori people as a *taonga*, or treasure. The Māori tell many stories about them. In some, the tuatara is fearsome. In others, they are considered guardians or keepers of knowledge. But Māori across the land seem to know that these creatures are special.

Among the world's most interesting survivors, their ancestors stretch back 250 million years. Can you imagine how many things have happened over that time? Ice ages have come and gone. Whole continents have changed shape, drifted apart and collided. Many species and groups of animals have emerged and gone extinct. But the tuatara is still here as the last of its kind.

Even individual tuatara live a surprisingly long time. One estimate is up to 137 years. They have very low metabolic rates, which means they move slowly and can go months without eating. Sitting outside their burrows, half hidden by a kaleidoscope of greenery in a thick New Zealand forest, they are patient, waiting for a bug to scuttle by. They seem to endure all of the ups and downs of their lives calmly, with little but a blink of the eye, an opening of the mouth, a slurp and crunch of a spider or seabird egg. They grow only to around a kilogram, but before the arrival of humans and small mammals like rats, which prey on them, they ruled their native land.

What can you teach us, tuatara, about how to survive? Enduring catastrophes, a world dimmed by dust and even the loss of most living beings, your ancestors carried on. Sometimes it's helpful to have a broader view. All things come and go. Life is always changing. Perhaps you can inspire us to meet the twists and turns of our own lives with balance and patience.

CROWS
know how to learn

Calm and pretty, high in a tree, a shiny black crow looks down from a regal perch. With one glossy eye, she watches, perhaps wondering what you're doing down there on the pavement. In return, maybe you wonder too . . . what's going on in that mind of hers? She's clearly paying attention, maybe learning something new, as she sits alert in the branches, patiently observing.

These extra-large songbirds of the corvid family are some of Earth's most intelligent beings, and one big reason for their cleverness is their ability to learn. Crows can pick out human faces and remember who's mean and who's nice. For one experiment, scientists wearing masks went out and caught some crows (which the birds really don't like). When the scientists returned with the masks, even several years later, crows recognized the masks and called out alarms – even crows who hadn't been there when the birds were caught. It turns out crows communicate about dangers and risks.

Crows can also make tools. In the South Pacific, New Caledonian crows like to eat insects out of trees, so they fashion hooks out of sticks to make foraging easier. Other crows adapt to new habitats like cities through creative problem-solving. Some drop unshelled nuts on roads and wait for passing cars to crush and crack them open. Still others have been seen pressing the button of a water fountain while another drinks. Crows have also been known to mimic words and sentences in human languages. In 1964, a crow in Missoula, Montana learned to say 'here, boy', and rounded up all the dogs in the neighbourhood.

Sometimes people, especially in Western cultures, think of crows as omens of death, maybe because they're cloaked in black and eat carcasses. But in other places, they are linked with wisdom and longevity. Like us, crows' secret to success is intelligence. Without any doubt, you are clever in your own unique way. You are good at learning, whether you pick up knowledge by listening, reading, observing or doing. If you ever forget your own genius and brightness, remember the crow, who sits so often unnoticed, but aware of everything around her.

Crows can recognize individual human voices and even notice the difference between languages.

OTTERS
know how to take care of their bodies

Floating in a bed of seaweed, drifting on sun-speckled swells, the sea otter is at home in the ocean. How can a mammal, with warm blood coursing through her veins and not a bit of blubber, survive these cool-water seas? Her gifts are her uniquely high metabolism and her famously dense fur. Her metabolism keeps her temperature high, and her two layers of fur provide warmth and waterproofing. With as many as 1 million hairs per square inch, sea otter fur is the thickest of all the world's mammals.

The otter's prized possession requires care and tending. Sea otters spend up to six hours a day grooming. Using her paws and claws, an otter combs and carefully picks out dirt and debris. She scratches her belly and rubs her face. She licks and pulls at her pelt, nosing and nuzzling.

She even blows warm air into her underfur, which gets trapped, forming a warm-air suit. An outer coat of slick guard hairs keeps out the cool water. With a limber body and loose skin, an otter can tend to every part of her body by herself. Still, for some otters, it's nice to have a little help. Pups aren't able to groom themselves, so for the first few months their mothers do it for them.

River otters are related but very different creatures, shooting through streams and freshwater lakes but also scampering on land. From the Eurasian otter to the giant otter of the Amazon, they too need to keep their fur healthy and clean. North American river otters, for example, have been seen rolling around on the ground or squeezing water from their fur by rubbing against a hard object, using it like a squeegee.

Chances are you don't have super-fur like the sea otter, but your one precious body needs care and attention too. Sometimes, we have to remember to stop and listen. What does your body need in this moment? Perhaps rest, warmth, moisture or movement. Or maybe, like the otter, it needs to be groomed. Whether you're brushing your teeth or floating in a bath, take your sweet time. There's no rush at all. Your body needs love, care and respect to thrive.

In some places, sea otters were hunted nearly to extinction for their fur. Now, many communities are growing.

sea otter

WHALE SHARKS
know how to be gentle

Diving under the swells of a quiet sea,
you slip into a realm of shades of blue –
filled with light, vast and deep.

The shadow of a giant appears in the distance,
her tail swaying back and forth with grace.
Swimming slowly,
she seems to be beyond worrying
about time or pace.

From her great square head, she eyes you,
but then passes by – huge and harmless.
Longer than a bus, and heavier too,
she is the biggest fish in all the ocean.

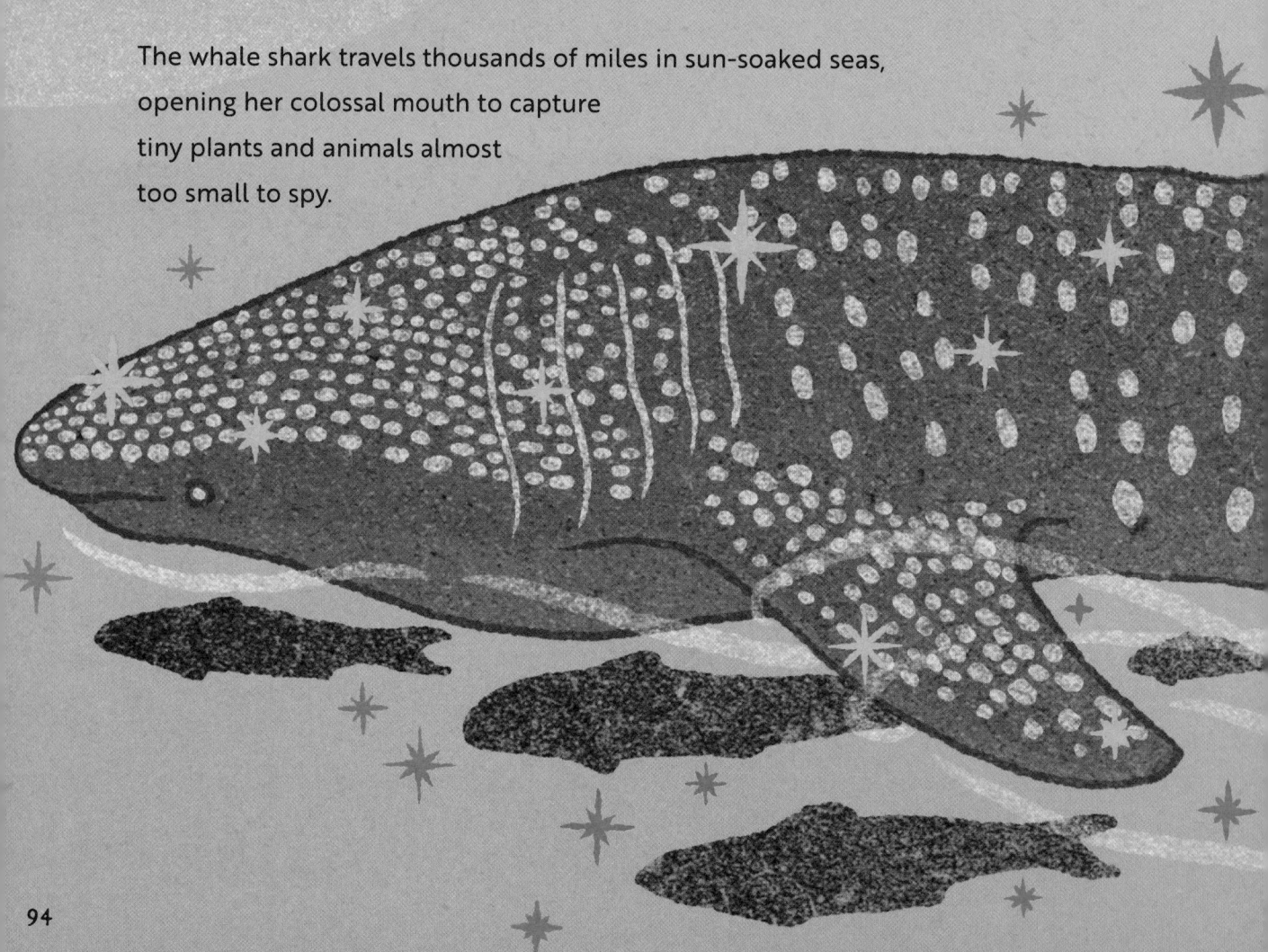

The whale shark travels thousands of miles in sun-soaked seas,
opening her colossal mouth to capture
tiny plants and animals almost
too small to spy.

In Indonesia, whale sharks are considered sacred,
peaceful protectors of the waters.
They are thought to have the spirit of grandmothers.
Being gentle can make you beloved.

How would it feel to be the world's largest fish,
a shark no less,
and yet be a safe presence for others?

Causing no harm, and free from regrets,
how sweet it would be
to swim through this world,
living in peace.

In the Swahili language of East Africa, whale sharks are called *papa shillingi*, or 'shark covered in coins'. It's said the creator and angels made the sharks' spots by covering them in gold and silver shillings (coins).

ANTS
know how to create great communities

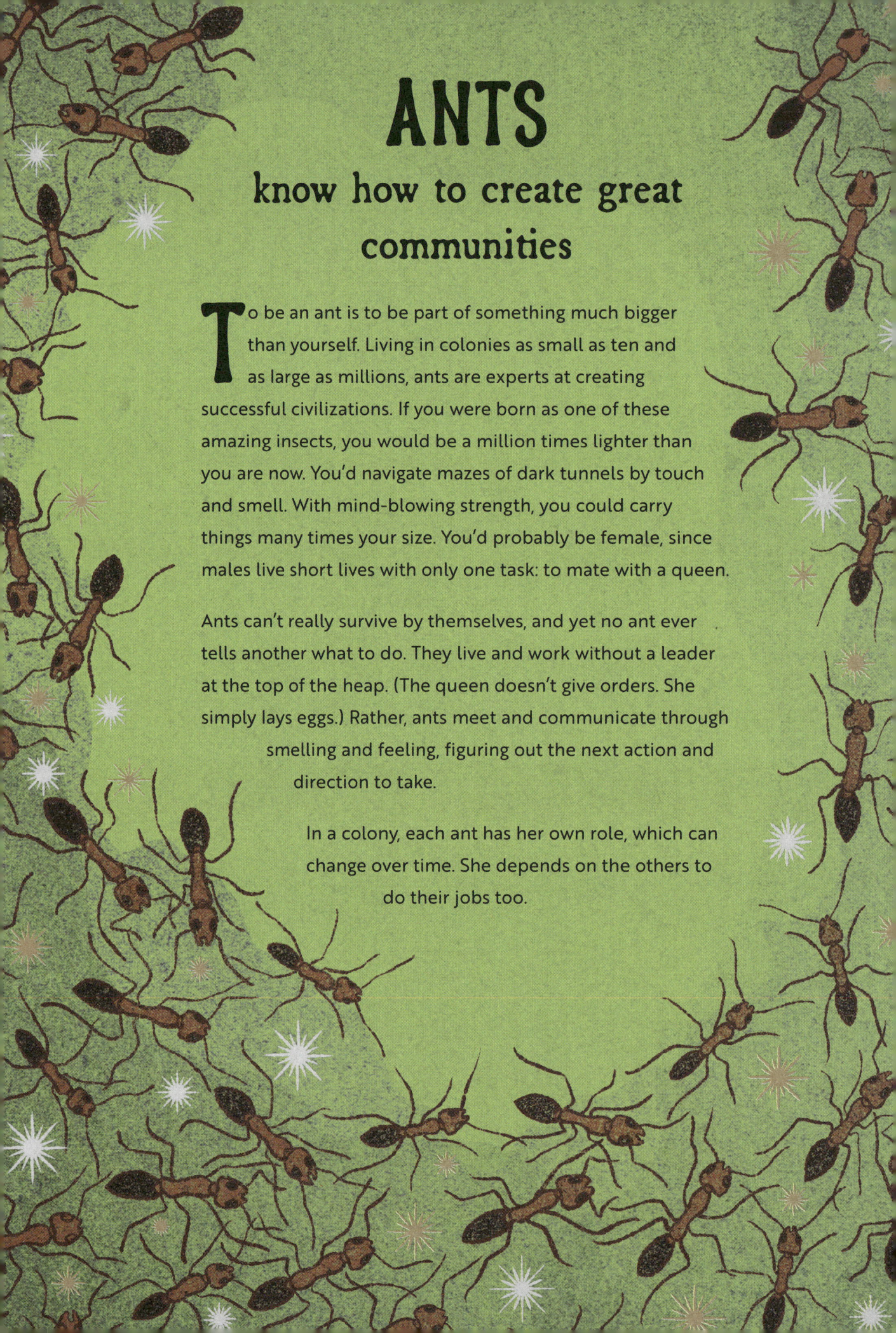

To be an ant is to be part of something much bigger than yourself. Living in colonies as small as ten and as large as millions, ants are experts at creating successful civilizations. If you were born as one of these amazing insects, you would be a million times lighter than you are now. You'd navigate mazes of dark tunnels by touch and smell. With mind-blowing strength, you could carry things many times your size. You'd probably be female, since males live short lives with only one task: to mate with a queen.

Ants can't really survive by themselves, and yet no ant ever tells another what to do. They live and work without a leader at the top of the heap. (The queen doesn't give orders. She simply lays eggs.) Rather, ants meet and communicate through smelling and feeling, figuring out the next action and direction to take.

In a colony, each ant has her own role, which can change over time. She depends on the others to do their jobs too.

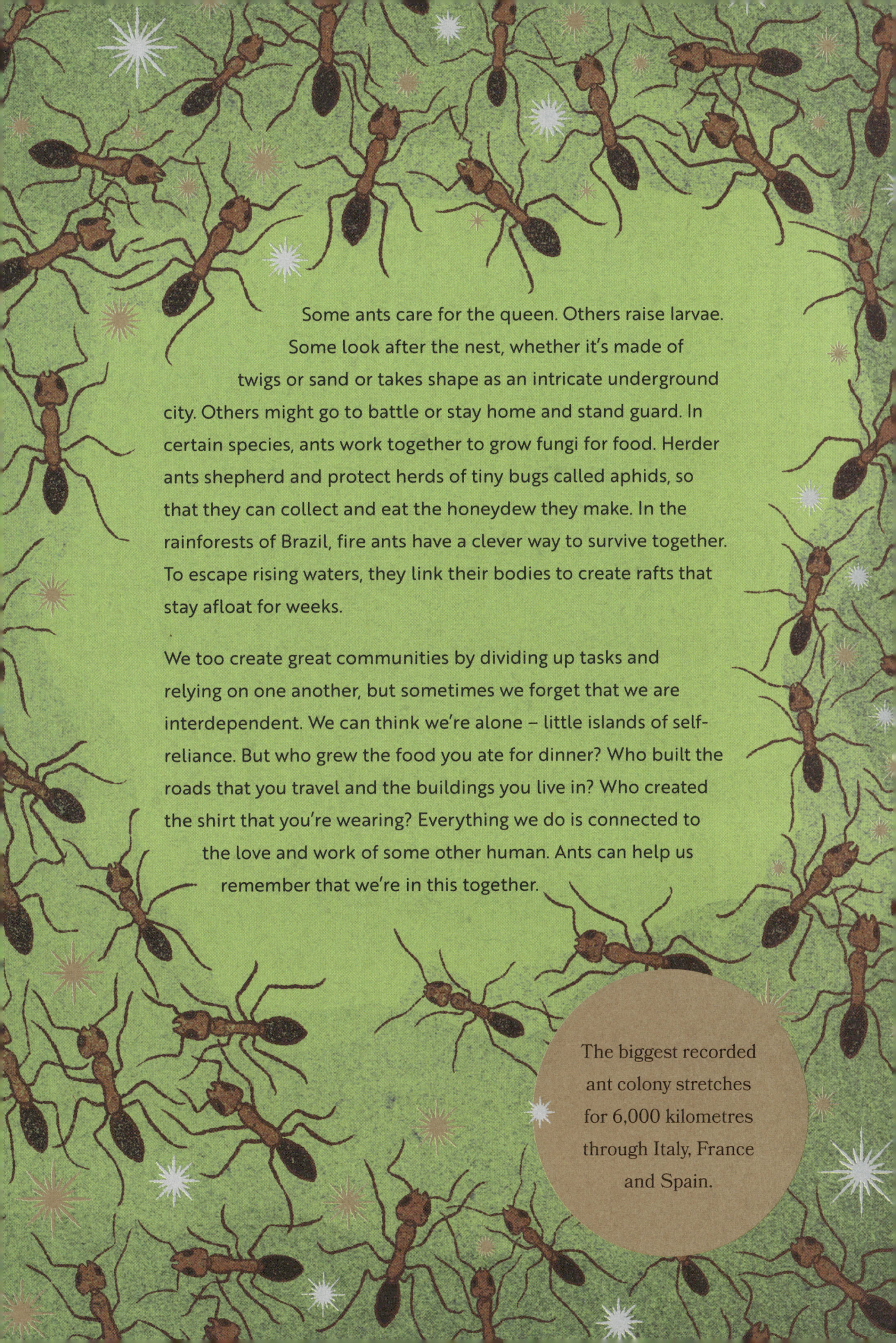

Some ants care for the queen. Others raise larvae. Some look after the nest, whether it's made of twigs or sand or takes shape as an intricate underground city. Others might go to battle or stay home and stand guard. In certain species, ants work together to grow fungi for food. Herder ants shepherd and protect herds of tiny bugs called aphids, so that they can collect and eat the honeydew they make. In the rainforests of Brazil, fire ants have a clever way to survive together. To escape rising waters, they link their bodies to create rafts that stay afloat for weeks.

We too create great communities by dividing up tasks and relying on one another, but sometimes we forget that we are interdependent. We can think we're alone – little islands of self-reliance. But who grew the food you ate for dinner? Who built the roads that you travel and the buildings you live in? Who created the shirt that you're wearing? Everything we do is connected to the love and work of some other human. Ants can help us remember that we're in this together.

The biggest recorded ant colony stretches for 6,000 kilometres through Italy, France and Spain.

BEES
know how to find their unique place in the world

It's spring in the forest and all around the sounds of rushing streams float through the trees. Feel the sun on your back. Breathe in the scents of wet soil and sweet blooms. Birds flit between branches, and everywhere you go, you hear the friendly buzz of the bees. Spring is their favourite time, you see. Dazzling flowers brighten the land – purple, blue, orange, white and red. The bees are flying great loops, arcs and lines as they journey near and far on their courageous quests for pollen and nectar.

Here's a marvellous secret to know about bees: only a few bee species out of 20,000 worldwide actually make honey. In fact, honey bees are the only ones who live in big colonies, work together and perform mysterious dances to share the location of flowers. The world of bees is even more wonderful and diverse than you may have ever known. Native bees roam every continent except Antarctica. There are even Arctic bumblebees, *Bombus polaris*, extra-furry fellows who live in the world's northernmost tundra. To prepare for flight, they get warm by shivering their muscles or sitting inside cone-shaped flowers that trap heat and light.

Wild bees nest in all sorts of places, like dead wood, plant stems, between rocks and in holes in the ground. From the highlands of Central Asia to the mountains of Spain, look into an abandoned snail shell and you just might spot a special mason bee who nests in quite an unusual nook! Some bees are as big as thumbs and others are as small as a grain of rice.

mason bee

You might recognize bees who have black and yellow stripes, but have you ever seen Australia's domino cuckoo bee, who is black with white dots and sneaks its eggs into others' nests? Or North America's blue orchard bee, who is metallic blue and pollinates orchard trees?

Many bees are uniquely adapted to gather pollen and nectar from just a few or even one native plant. There are blueberry bees and globe mallow bees and bees who visit spiky desert cactuses. There are bees in the tropics who glide through the moonlight looking for night-blooming flowers. There are squash and gourd bees who pollinate vegetables and melons – the males, who don't nest, can sometimes be found fast asleep in big blossoms.

It seems there's a niche for every type of bee, a unique purpose and place to be. And while we may have very different lives than our friends the bees, it turns out the same is true for people too – there's a unique place and role on this earth for each and every one of us. You fit perfectly into this world like a piece in a puzzle, and without you, it would be a very different place.

domino cuckoo bee

Bees are renowned for their powers of pollination. More than 80 per cent of the world's plants depend on their work.

BATS
know how to be quiet heroes

In the tranquil dusk, lie on your back in a field and stare straight up as the sun says goodbye and the moon starts to rise. Mysterious beings are here in your midst. Blink and you'll miss them – bats, the fastest mammals on Earth and messengers of evening. Their spiky silhouettes flash across a violet sky. Quick as a blaze, here and then not, circling, swooping, dipping and diving, bats are wizards of shadows and darkness.

Some people fear bats for their night-dwelling ways, linking them with vampires, death and the devil. Sometimes they're seen as symbols of the underworld. But the ancient Maya revered them as mystical symbols of fertility. The Chinese link them with good fortune and happiness, and ancient Macedonians carried their bones as good luck charms called amulets.

Whether you smile or tremble when you meet a bat (or a few), one thing is certainly true: bats are generous givers and secret heroes. Vampire bats live in groups and feed by licking drops of blood from small cuts they make in animals' skin. If one bat hasn't found a meal, another will vomit up blood and share it with them.

bumblebee bat

The world's tiniest bat is the bumblebee bat, as big as a fingernail. The largest bat, a flying fox, has a wingspan of up to 1.5 metres.

Just by being who they are and doing what they do, bats bestow blessings on us too. In search of nectar, some bats drink from flowers and pollinate crops and other plants, like bananas, avocados and mangoes.

Many bats eat fruit, and because they fly (and poo!) all around, they scatter seeds all over the land. In some young forests, bats are responsible for rooting 95 per cent of new plants. Without the work of bug-eating bats, we'd have piles of pests too. Some eat as many as ten mosquitoes or fourteen fruit flies each minute, and others slurp up so many shiny insects that their poo, called guano, actually sparkles.

Bats may not even know that they are helping others. They're just living their lives and don't need fanfare or awards. Reflecting on the ways of these creatures of night, may we all contribute to the wellbeing of others and share the things we cherish. Even if our acts of giving are unseen under the cover of darkness, we can be thoughtful and generous through quiet heroics.

flying fox

KOALAS
know how to sleep

In a fragrant eucalyptus wood
in southeast Australia, look up to see
the much-beloved bum of the big-eared one.

The koala survives entirely on leaves
and doesn't have a whole lot of energy,
which is why he has an amazing talent:
the ability to sleep!

Nestled in the crook of a gum tree,
all curled up in the cold,
or limbs a-hanging on a steamy evening,
the koala snoozes at least eighteen hours a day.

Sleep, the peaceable koala seems to know,
is the secret to the good life.
It allows him to renew both body and spirit.

For all creatures big and small,
the time eventually comes
to surrender to slumber.

Find yourself a safe perch,
far from hubbub and harm,
a sanctuary or shelter –
your version of a great tree.

Cosy under a blanket of stars,
unburden yourself of worries.

Like the heavy-lidded koala,
drift off into dreamland –
the magical realm of the restful beyond.

THE GIFT OF BEING HUMAN

Just like all of the creatures in this book and across the planet, we humans are animals too. We breathe and move. We take in food, air and light. Even if we don't hear like an owl, see like a fly or have the sensitive skin of a frog, we sense the world around us in astonishing detail. We too have gifts to share with our fellow citizens of Earth.

With our big brains, we have the gift of curiosity and the ability to learn. With our social ways, we can live and work together, cooperating to create dazzling civilizations. With our big hearts, we have the ability to love, to help each other and to care.

Sometimes, however, we forget our best qualities. As a species, we have caused damage. We have hogged Earth's lands and waters so other animals don't have enough space. We have burned so much energy the climate is warming. We have polluted the air, sea and land. We haven't always lived up to our greatest potential.

But don't despair! Remember the most important gift that we have: the incredible ability to make good decisions. Our unique and gorgeous planet needs us to recall the best of who we are. So let's focus our abilities to love, to learn, to care for others and to live and work together.

We can learn from the wisdom of animals and be inspired by humans who are leading the way. We too can live in harmony and make the world a more beautiful place.

Across the world, people have saved species from the brink of extinction by breeding them in captivity, reintroducing them into the wild and protecting them as they roam. Now, many animal populations are recovering, including the Iberian lynx in Spain and Portugal, the giant panda in China and grey wolves in the United States.

During and after World War II, people across the planet used the pesticide DDT to kill nuisance bugs like mosquitoes and protect crops. It turned out that the chemical collected in soil and insects. When the birds ate the insects, the toxic substance built up in their bodies and the number of songbirds and raptors tumbled. Luckily, people noticed and cared. Many countries banned DDT in the 1970s and many bird species have recovered.

Human beings have hunted whales for food and materials for thousands of years. But in the 19th and 20th centuries, so many were hunted that some species were nearly wiped out. In the late 20th century, nations banded together to curb hunting and create sanctuaries. Simply by letting them live, species such as humpback, fin, sei and blue whales made incredible comebacks all on their own.

CARING FOR OUR FAMILY OF BEINGS

While there are many ways animals can help and inspire us, we have the ability to help wildlife too. Sharing our love for them and letting them live their natural lives is a great start. If a spider has taken residence in your home, for example, you can gently catch and release it outside using a cup and a piece of paper. Here are some more ways you can be a friend to animals.

Plant a Pollinator Garden

Across the world, people create beautiful outdoor spaces, large and small, that are rich in plants beloved by pollinators. You too can find out what flowers local bees, birds and butterflies love, then plant them in your garden, in pots or in a window box. Sit back and enjoy the buzz and bustle of a healthy ecosystem!

Create a Home for Wildlife

Some species appreciate a helping hand when it comes to homebuilding. For bats and other wildlife, leave dead standing trees, logs, shrubs and leaves right where they are to make cosy habitats. Or look up local bird species that like human-built homes and find out what you could create for them: a birdhouse, a nesting shelf, a platform?

Turn Off the Lights

Since the beginning of time, wildlife and plants have navigated life by the cycles of light and dark. Light pollution from our homes and cities threatens those cycles. You can lead the way by only using the lights you really need and turning them off when not in use. See if you can shield, dim or point your outdoor lighting downward. You'll make a difference for many species and enjoy more stars (and maybe fireflies!) too.

Be a Trash Wizard

Even picking up one piece of trash from the sidewalk can save a marine animal like a sea turtle or albatross from accidentally swallowing it or getting caught in it. Even better, grab some gloves and trash bags, spread the word to friends and family, and gather for a beach or river clean-up party!

Take Down Sporting Nets

Young owls and other birds often get tangled up in football nets, string lights and similar equipment as they learn to hunt. You can help by rolling up your football, volleyball and other nets at night and taking down unused home decorations, such as Christmas lights or fake Halloween spider webs.

Decorate Your Windows

Birds haven't evolved to see the perfectly clear surface of windows. They often accidentally fly into glass, injuring or even killing themselves. (By one estimate, up to a billion birds die this way every year in the United States alone.) Decorate the outside of your biggest windows with removable decals that help them see the glass and you could save a songbird's life!

Become a Citizen Scientist

From counting critters in your area to gathering samples of water or soil, you can use your powers of observation, identification, collection and even photography to contribute to important science. You don't need special qualifications, just enthusiasm and time. Look up citizen science projects in your area through local organizations, websites like citizenscience.gov (in the United States) or zooniverse.org, or an association devoted to protecting an animal you love.

INDEX

adapting 9, 78–81, 82, 90, 99
Africa 35, 37, 44, 56, 57, 66, 78
   East 64, 95
Ainu 42
Akbar 15
amphibians
   frogs 82–3, 104
animal
   babies and young 20, 25, 35, 36, 40, 54, 57, 66, 107
   groups 35, 51, 57, 68, 70, 86, 100
   homes see habitats, homes
   types see amphibians, birds, fish, invertebrates, mammals, reptiles
Anishinaabe 70
Antarctica 66, 78, 84, 85, 98
Arctic 78, 84, 85, 98
Asia 18, 44, 49, 57, 72, 78
   Central 98
   South 15, 39
Australia 54, 69, 99, 102
Aztecs 40

being yourself 22–3, 27, 50–51
   see also uniqueness
belonging 15, 68–9
bioluminescence 23
birds 20, 69, 105, 106, 107
   Arctic terns 84–5
   crows 8, 90–91,
   eagles 17, 41, 72–3
   flamingos 50–51
   hummingbirds 40–41
   owls 10–11, 104, 107
   penguins 66–7
   pigeons 14–15
   vultures 44–45
bonding 20, 86
Brazil 97
breathing 11, 20, 39, 82, 104
   to calm down 17, 49
British Isles 37

California 58
calmness 48–9
camouflage 76
   see also mimicry
Canada 58

caring 35, 57, 58, 66, 92–3, 97, 104, 106–7
Central America 17
China 24, 25, 57, 65
cleaning 44–5, 74–5, 92–3, 107
cleverness see intelligence
climate change 42, 104
communication 35, 86, 90, 96
conservation 24, 105–7
creativity 18–19, 90
curiosity 26, 53, 86, 104

devotion 66, 107
Diné 18
dinosaurs 27, 88
disease 30, 45

eggs 30, 58, 66, 89, 96, 99
Egypt, ancient 15, 57
emotions 35, 86
endangered animals 82
England 12
Eurasia 72
Europe 11, 18, 44, 49, 70, 72
extinction 88, 89, 93, 105

families 56, 58, 59, 66, 70, 90
fierceness 24, 25, 40–41, 54
fish 20, 27, 53, 66, 85
   salmon 42
   whale sharks 94–5
flying 11, 30, 31, 40, 50, 58, 85, 98, 101, 107
food 12, 30, 39, 54, 57, 66, 69, 72, 97, 104, 105
France 39, 70, 97

Galapagos Islands 66
genes 42
gentleness 9, 24, 25, 94–5
Germany 70, 73
gods and goddesses 11, 20, 27, 46, 57
Greece 70
Greeks, ancient 20
grooming 86, 92–3
growth 47, 52–3, 64, 69, 76, 89

habitats 82, 90, 106
   cities 8, 10, 12, 80, 90, 107

deserts 10, 11, 36, 69, 78, 80, 99
forests and woods 10, 12, 19, 22, 24, 36, 38, 39, 42, 48, 49, 54, 58, 62, 64, 70, 80, 86, 89, 98, 101, 102
   see also rainforests
grasslands, plains and savannahs 35, 36, 47, 56, 64, 80, 86
jungles 69, 78
lakes 48, 93
meadows 10, 11
mountains 24, 36, 45, 58, 69, 98
oceans and seas 20, 26, 27, 32, 33, 42, 52, 53, 66, 74, 75, 85, 92, 94, 105
ponds 18
rainforests 12, 17, 72, 97
reefs 26, 27, 53
rivers and streams 18, 19, 42, 45, 76, 82, 93, 98, 107
swamps 82
tundra 36, 80, 98
wetlands 10
Haudenosaunee 58
Hawai'i 27
hearing 10–11, 14, 35, 48, 52, 58, 63, 70, 78, 98, 104
hibernation 39
Hittites 57
homes 12, 14, 15, 24, 106, 107
   dens 12, 38, 39
   nests 66, 97, 98, 99
homing instinct 14
hunting 11, 20, 27, 48, 57, 66, 70, 72, 76, 78, 107
   by humans 93, 105

Indonesia 27, 95
intelligence 12, 17, 27, 39, 90–91, 97
invertebrates 27, 52
   ants 96–7
   bees 98–9, 106
   butterflies 58–61, 106
   crickets 18, 62–3
   fireflies 22–3, 107
   flies 30–31, 45, 101, 104

jellyfish 32–3
lobsters 52–3
octopuses 26–9, 53
oysters 26, 74–5
slugs and snails 8, 26, 68–9, 98
spiders 8, 18–19, 89, 106
Italy 97

Japan 37, 42, 78

Kiribati 18
Klamath 42

learning 18, 20, 26, 30, 47, 54, 66, 70, 75, 86, 90, 104
letting go 46–7
listening see hearing

Maasai 56, 57
Macedonians 100
Madagascar 19
Maine 48
Makah 42
mammals 31, 35, 37, 38, 69, 72, 89, 92, 100
   bats 100–101, 106
   bears 24–5, 38–9
   chimpanzees 86–7
   dolphins 20–21
   foxes 8, 72, 78–81
   hares 36–7, 72
   humans 11, 19, 20, 24, 25, 27, 31, 37, 39, 42, 45, 48, 54, 57, 70, 89, 90, 91, 97, 104–105
   koalas 102–103
   lions 24, 56–7
   otters 92–3
   sloths 17, 72
   squirrels 12
   Tasmanian devils 54
   whales 105
   wolves 70–71, 105
Māori 89
marsupials 54
mating 24, 42, 52, 63, 69, 71, 96
Maya, ancient 100
Mazahua 59
memory 12, 35, 90
Mesopotamia 15
Mexico 40, 58, 59, 73
migration 42, 58, 85
mimicry 19, 27, 90
molluscs 26

Montana 90
moulting 46–7, 53
movement 17, 20, 30–31, 32, 37, 42, 72, 89, 93, 104
   fast see speed
   slow see slowness
Mozambique 105

Namibia 73, 82
Navajo see Diné
New Caledonia 90
New Guinea 65
New Zealand 66, 89
North America 11, 27, 37, 39, 42, 44, 49, 58, 70, 72, 78, 93, 99

omens see symbolism

patience 49, 78, 89, 90
peacefulness 14, 24, 95
peacemaking 86
perseverance 9, 42, 84
Peru 72
Philippines 65, 72
Pima 11
playing 20–21, 27, 70
poisons 82–3
pollination 30, 99, 101, 106
Portugal 49, 105
predators 19, 42, 47, 53, 66, 68, 69, 70, 72, 82
prey 19, 27, 49, 57, 72, 77, 78, 89
problem solving 20, 27, 90
protection 24, 57, 64–5, 66, 70, 82, 95, 97, 105, 107
Purépecha 59

Quileute 42

remembering see memory
reptiles 82, 88, 89
   crocodiles 76–7
   snakes 14, 27, 46–7
   tortoises and turtles 64–5, 107
   tuatara 88–9
   see also dinosaurs
Rome, ancient 15, 46, 73

Sami 42
Scandinavia 27, 42
seasons 12, 39, 84
   autumn 12, 38
   spring 24, 64, 98

summer 22, 85
winter 12, 36, 38, 66
seeing 11, 31, 35, 47, 48, 68, 72, 77, 104, 107
Senegal 86
senses see hearing, seeing, smell, taste, touch
sensitivity 35, 82–3, 104
Seychelles 65
Sicily 11
singing 62–3, 67
skin shedding 46–7
sleep 17, 99, 102–103
slowness 17, 31, 35, 39, 44, 47, 64, 68, 89, 94
smell 15, 35, 42, 44, 68, 96
South Africa 47
South America 17, 19, 37, 39, 44, 66, 78
Spain 49, 97, 98, 105
speed 30, 31, 36–7, 72, 100
stillness 17, 36, 76–7
stories 18, 27, 37, 48, 59, 70, 89
strength 27, 35, 41, 42, 54, 56–7, 70, 72, 73, 76, 85, 96
symbolism 11, 20, 24, 25, 27, 30, 45, 73, 90, 100

Tahiti 20
Thailand 12
tales see stories
Tanzania 86
Tasmania 54
taste 68
teamwork 9, 19, 57, 70–71, 72, 96–97, 98, 104,
tools, using 27, 86, 90
touch 35, 96
trying again see perseverance
Turkey 57, 70

Umpqua 42
uniqueness 19, 27, 63, 64, 68, 83, 90, 92, 98–9, 104
   see also being yourself
United States 18, 105
Utes 39

vision see seeing
volcanoes 18

working together see teamwork
World War II 15, 105